NOTES ON SUICIDE

Simon Critchley is Hans Jonas Professor of Philosophy at the New School for Social Research in New York. His books include *Very Little... Almost Nothing*, *Infinitely Demanding*, *The Book of Dead Philosophers*, *The Faith of the Faithless*, and *Tragedy, The Greeks and Us*. He has also written short books on David Bowie and football, and a novella called *Memory Theatre* (also published by Fitzcarraldo Editions). He runs 'The Stone', a philosophy column in *The New York Times* and is also 50 per cent of an obscure musical combo called Critchley & Simmons. A new book, *Bald*, is forthcoming.

'No one ever lacks a good reason for suicide, wrote Cesare Pavese. With passionate lucidity and philosophical intelligence, Simon Critchley explores what these reasons might be, bracketing simple moral judgement and trying to fight his way past the social, psychical and existential blockages that inhibit us whenever we try to think about this ever-baffling issue.'
— Lars Iyer, author of *Wittgenstein Jr*

'We must talk about suicide without shame or sanctimony. This book is a good place to start.'
— Max Liu, *Independent*

'This intense book is an instance of thought born in the hour of anguish, which eloquently makes the case for suicide not as an act to be pitilessly condemned, but a possibility for which any of us might be thankful.'
— Rob Doyle, *Irish Times*

'It is a willingness to accommodate ambiguity that gives *Notes on Suicide* its quiet moral authority; Critchley is generous without being platitudinous, rigorous but not overbearing. Remarkably for a disquisition on self-killing, one comes away from it feeling curiously chipper.'
— Houman Barekat, *Vol. 1 Brooklyn*

'*Notes on Suicide* examines the sociological and literary history of the act, before performing an unflinching self-examination of Critchley's own relationship with the choice between life and death.'
— Rosie Clarke, *Music & Literature*

'*Notes on Suicide* shows us not how to understand, but how to realise what we don't know, can never know, and what it is to deal with that awareness.'
— Cal Revely-Calder, *3:AM*

Fitzcarraldo Editions

NOTES ON SUICIDE

SIMON CRITCHLEY

Followed by

OF SUICIDE by DAVID HUME

Preface

When I wrote *Notes on Suicide*, my aim was simple: to try and open up a space for thinking about suicide as a free act; and to expand, as far as I could, the vocabulary for such thinking.

Suicide is a topic that invites strong, indeed panicked and confused, reactions. So, in order to find leeway for the kind of space I was imagining, some ground had to be cleared. I had become increasingly frustrated by the limited and predictable ways in which suicide and suicides were discussed, both in the news and public debate, but also among friends and acquaintances. It seemed as if we suffered from a genuine impoverishment of language and compassionately minded clear thinking on the topic. Even worse, my own ruminations on suicide were mired in the same muddiness and limitation. I decided to try and do something about it in the way I know best, in writing.

I had become fascinated in why it was that many people saw suicide as somehow wrong, as the expression of a moral failure, a life somehow gone awry, and which gave rise to the most peculiar and powerful reactions of upset, outrage, voluble gossip or, quite often and oddly, stubborn silence. I began to look into the historic reasons that lie behind the prohibition against suicide. As I read about it more carefully, I became increasingly convinced that the moral and legal framing of the prohibition against suicide had its roots in the idea of suicide as a sin. This idea can be traced to medieval Christian theology and metaphysics, specifically the claim that life is a gift from God which grants us the right of use, but not the right of governance or dominion over our lives. To kill oneself is to assume a power over life that does not lie with us, but only with the deity, however the latter might be conceived. Although arguably only a small fraction of people still holds such Christian metaphysics to be true, it nonetheless has enduring effects on our moral and legal thinking about suicide, giving rise to extreme and confused reactions.

Once the theological history of the prohibition against suicide has been better understood and unravelled, it becomes easier to show how the secular discussion of suicide in terms of rights and duties is often misplaced and conceptually incoherent. This is what I try and do in the longish second part of the essay. But I also criticize the libertarian argument for suicide, which turns on questionable assumptions about rationality and autonomy. I am deeply opposed to any argument that the sovereignty of God, monarch, country or community should be the basis for a prohibition of suicide. I am also suspicious of claims to self-sovereignty that support any right to suicide as a simple rational choice or self-evident civic liberty. So much for the polemical part of the essay.

I then turn to suicide notes and try to examine them, with deliberate coldness, as a distinct and compelling literary genre. Not all suicides leave notes – many don't – and their reliability can be easily questioned, given that they often follow quite predictable, indeed stereotypical rhetorical patterns. And yet they are crucial evidence for the extreme mental distress and incontrovertible tunnel-vision experienced by the suicidally depressed. They also exercise a peculiar fascination on the living and have an almost pornographic appeal that draws readers in, myself included. As Kay Redfield Jamison writes, 'The particulars of suicide hook our imagination in a dark way.' This is hardly wholesome, but it is a phenomenon that merits careful attention. For me, the most powerful feature of suicide notes is the way in which they make manifest the extraordinary psychical ambivalence of depressive isolation and extreme exhibitionism of masochism and sadism, and, most importantly, hatred and love. In suicide notes, the most intense self-hatred gives rise to the most radical exclamations of love.

From there, I look into suicide as a vehicle of revenge, as a way of giving voice to persecutory fantasies of victimization and narcissistic self-justification. Here we confront the disturbing phenomenon of homicide-suicide in cases like the Sandy Hook Elementary School shooting of 2012 and, more particularly the case of Elliot Rodger, who killed himself after killing six people in California in 2014, leaving behind a lengthy manifesto and a disturbing video suicide note. Since the time of writing, Rodger has become a hero of the INCEL (involuntary celibate) movement, an online subculture of often reactionary and consistently misogynistic young men, which has been behind a significant number of killings since 2014.

In the final part of the essay, I consider the following question: what if suicide is not the unasked-for consequence of a psychopathological condition with a possibly organic basis, but is chosen as a free act, as an end in itself? How might we think about suicide when there is no apparent motivating cause? If such a thing is possible – and it clearly is – then it leads everyone to ask themselves the question: why live? Here I very consciously move into the area of existential analysis, which is perhaps not surprising since I think of myself as an existential phenomenologist, and work through a number of examples and texts by authors such as Edouard Levé, Albert Camus and Jean Améry. I try to think through the question of why it is that suicide seems so morally rebarbative, and face up to what Levé calls its scandalous beauty. *Homo sapiens* is distinguished by the capacity for self-slaughter, which is perhaps the price that we pay for self-consciousness, in particular the forms of acute self-consciousness characteristic of some writers, artists and scientists. It is essential to our sense of ourselves, others and the world that we face up to the experience of finitude that the question of suicide raises.

At every single moment we live and breathe, the arms for our self-destruction lie in our hands. Not that I am counselling in any way that we take up those arms against ourselves. On the contrary. I finish the essay by leaning on the wonderfully comic pessimism of Cioran, namely his notion that the problem with the suicidally depressed is that they are too optimistic. Nothing will be saved by taking our own lives, and a belief in suicide as the only way out derives from an arrogant over-estimation of our capacity for salvation through self-destruction. Therefore, why not stay awhile and enjoy the tender indifference of the world that holds itself out for our attention and our seemingly infinite capacity for disappointment? I end the essay with what we might think of as the pessimist's refutation of suicide, but this is a pessimism of strength, good humour and, hopefully, even high spirits. The question of the meaning of life is the wrong question and I humbly suggest that we stop asking it. Our minds will never stop rummaging through the drawers of self-doubt, self-disgust and self-pity in order to find some piece of forgotten dirty moral laundry. What is important is the ability to get life to stand still in order to look at it tenderly and with care, to cultivate slower forms of attention without renouncing life in some sovereign violent act. One should go on.

¶ I do not think that I am necessarily right in my views on suicide, nor do I think that I am particularly well-qualified to give them. What the reader will find in the following essay are impressions based on observation and reading. Nothing more. Those looking for real expertise in the psychopathology and neurobiology of suicidal depression can look elsewhere, for example in the writings of Redfield Jamison, such as the *Night Falls Fast*. Rather, this essay is what I wrote after I took myself off to the Brudenell Hotel in Aldeburgh on the Suffolk coast in November 2014. In retrospect, this seems like a very odd thing to do (in fact, writing during the Covid-19 summer in New York, going anywhere at the moment seems like an odd thing to do). The location now also seems more than a little self-dramatizing, with all those references to the vast North Sea. All I can say in my defence is that it didn't at the time. It felt like a logical decision to have made by someone who was struggling with what we might call the pains of love and a feeling of life's disintegration.

I won't engage in self-critique here, as it would take far too long and deflect from my purpose in writing this preface. But I am unhappy with the last pages of the essay, which I think move too quickly towards an upbeat conclusion in a way that seems slightly insouciant now. I don't think I really resolve the question of how love might be a force that can both pull us beyond any desire for self-slaughter, but also drive us into the depths of hatred and despair. I also think that I make heavy weather of the standard arguments around suicide in Part Two and the writing could be crisper and faster. To be brutally honest, I also felt a little skewered by one reviewer's questioning of the sincerity of my suicidal ideation, mainly because it led me to question my own sincerity in writing what I did at the time. What can I say? I was navigating rough waters at the time, but they feel less rough now, and I wonder whether there was a storm at sea at all.

I have backed off from talking publicly about suicide in recent years, partly because I think I have said what I wanted to say, but more importantly because I am slightly fearful of the strange, attractive energy that the topic can provoke in audiences, and I worried that it was getting too easy to both arouse and incite audiences while increasingly doubting my intentions in the process. The better I got at talking about suicide, the more fraudulent I felt in doing so. At times, I had the sense that I was running through a tried, trusted but tired stand-up routine that felt increasingly distant even as I was performing it.

That said, I'd like to think about whether anything has changed with respect to the question of suicide in the years since I wrote this essay. There is, obviously, the vast issue of climate collapse, and the fact that we are all engaged in a slow(ish) act of collective suicide, like a stoned business executive tottering and teetering atop of a high office building. There is the widely reported theme of 'deaths of despair' in the work of Anne Case and Angus Deaton, which compellingly documents the rise in self-destructive and suicidal behaviour, particularly among white working-class people without a college degree in the USA.

Of particular interest is the question of social media and whether there is a relation of causation or at least correlation between social media use and a range of behaviours, from mood disorders, to self-harm, suicidal ideation and suicide. I am not a social scientist and it would be slightly laughable if I presented myself as such. In my initial research for the essay, I carefully gathered a large number of sociological factoids about suicide which made it into my first draft, but which I then cut because I didn't feel confident about the truthfulness of what I was saying. It is very easy to give in to a kind of moral panic around suicide when it is linked to statistics, brightly coloured graphs and speculation about new patterns of destructive social behaviour, and it is very important not to give in to such panic. This is the stuff of the news cycle.

Any full understanding of suicide requires, at the very least, the cultivation of a much longer and broader view of suicidal behaviour across as wide a historical and cultural sweep as possible, along with the richest possible sociological data. It should also be informed by literary analysis, the vast archive of poetry, stories and movies at our fingertips. It also needs to be particularly sensitive to how suicidal behaviour maps onto gender arrangements in various societies and to try and analyze clearly how suicide affects men and women in very different ways and, in particular, the proclivities towards suicide among non-binary and transgender people. Analogous considerations would have to apply to questions of ethnicity and race in relation to suicide. And, importantly, a consideration of these issues cannot exclude the question of whether and to what extent suicidal behaviour has an organic, biological basis. Are suicidal patterns of behaviour best explained organically in terms of neurobiology and, even, serotonin levels? Is suicidality even an inheritable condition within, say, certain families and communities? Is suicide to be explained through some mixture of nature and nurture where the precise weight of each side of the scale is very much in the balance? I simply do not know the answers to these questions and lack the expertise to make any sort of helpful and informed judgement. As I already said, my approach to suicide is more philosophical and my inclination is towards existential analyses of the topic.

Yet the question of social media has me worried because the early indications from the research are genuinely disturbing. I'd like to lean a little on the ongoing, extensive work of Jonathan Haidt and Jean Twenge, which is a tremendously helpful compilation of a number of studies, mainly focused in the English-speaking world. The research is beginning to show that the effects of social media use are serious, far-reaching and are getting worse; worse for females than males; and worse still for young females. In response to the question: has there been a significant increase in incidences of mood disorders, self-harm, suicidal ideation and suicide since 2010? Then the answer is yes. The causes here can be social, such as shifts in parenting practices, from absent parents leaving the care of children to nannies or whoever, to helicopter parents who overlook every detail of their children's existence and drown it out with the overbearing noise of their care. The causes can also be socio-economic, for example the effects of the so-called Great Recession of 2007-9. But there is no doubt that a prime cause is the rapid and incredibly widespread adoption of smartphones and the spread of social media.

There has been a spectacular increase in the occurrence of major depressive episodes (MDEs) in recent years. Although this can be detected across a wide number of age groups, the behavioural effects of social media use on the experience of depression are particularly marked among Gen Z or what Twenge calls iGen (internet generation), namely those born between roughly 1995 and 2015, who reached adolescence after

16

the adoption of smartphones. According to Haidt and Twenge (although this view has been challenged), if the period from 2000 to 2012 is compared to 2012 onwards, the time when smartphones achieved market saturation, then there has been a really significant rise in a number of behaviours, such as the frequency of suicidal ideation, the levels of suicide attempts, and the number of completed suicides. They claim that the suicide rate for pre-teen girls has doubled since 2012. And the rise in suicide rates among teenage girls is particularly striking and disturbing. Multiple anecdotes from families and friends, and the stories that pepper the new cycle would seem to confirm this trend. Again, the tendency towards moral panic should be avoided. There is simply no denying that something is changing and has changed in how we behave and how we feel, and that is due, in large part, to the massive use of smartphones. The effects of those changes are particularly and acutely marked among the young, especially young women. We need to pay careful attention to it.

It is excessive to speak of a 'suicide generation' among the young, but the increase in everything on the range from mood disorder to completed suicide is not simply random. It is notoriously hard to establish precise relations of causation between new technologies and social behaviours, in this case between social media and suicide. If such relations of causation were clearly established and became the dominant view, then (to put it rather mildly) this would be rather bad news for the business model of the immense social media companies that dominate our lives ('Use more Instagram. It kills your kids.') There is undisputedly a correlation between social media use and suicidal feelings and behaviour. Whether there is a will to actually do something about it, at the level of legislation and regulation at a governmental and trans-governmental level, is quite another matter.

¶ Leaving to one side the empirical data and thinking more at the level of personal feeling and intuition, we know that something is deeply wrong in our relation to social media. We sense it, we see it all the time, we smell it in the air. Regardless of the devastation that they are wreaking on our political institutions and the free flow of opinion apparently so cherished by our formerly liberal democracies, we know that Facebook, Instagram and the rest negatively affect our well-being. We know that after long periods of distracting, vicarious social media stimulation, our mood deteriorates, and we slump into a sleepless, agitated inertia. Passive social media use (called PSMU in some of the literature) induces fatigue, loneliness, depression, a kind of seventeenth-century Pascalian *ennui*, and the sense that our lives are inadequate and pointless in comparison to the manufactured glamour, righteous moralized rage and simple falsehood that stares back at us continuously from our tiny screens in an uninterrupted, rising flood tide. As Virginia Heffernan rightly puts it, we're all suffering from *hyper-arousal* and *hyper-lexia*, reading continuously and allowing ourselves to become incited and excited over and over again, before slipping back into exhausted amnesia. It is not just that we are bullied by social media (although many individuals are). It is rather that we allow and want ourselves to be bullied, to be subjected to a kind of passive beating, where everything and everyone are too much, and we watch an endless gallery of the immemorable move past our eyes from our Crusoesque, peopleless kingdoms of loneliness.

We are addicted to social media, and once addicted everything flows down an algorithmically generated gutter of links into a bottomless rabbit hole of melancholia. The effects of such addiction are isolation, agitation, fear, weird hypochondriac symptoms, insomnia and Hamlet-like inner-spiralling self-doubt. The depressive inferences of such behaviour are not hard to see or to imagine. Their implications for suicidal behaviour appear plain. Especially when our social media habits are combined with increased drug and alcohol dependency. The use of intoxicants here is in no way transgressive or experimental, but simply a way of getting through, of buttressing a deadening routine. Many of us feel like shit quite a lot of the time. Oddly, we seem to like it, or to behave in ways that make it worse.

All of these tendencies have been accelerated and exaggerated by the Covid-19 pandemic. The gangplanks of social interaction, shared ways of life and actual human contact that we took for granted have been pulled away. Other people are possible sources of contagion, and so are we. We advance masked and keep our distance. The pandemic has left us more reliant upon and exposed to the pervasive presence of digital existence. To use the ghastly lingo, Covid-19 feels like one long MDE exacerbated by PSMU. As for the effects of the Covid-19 pandemic on the varieties of mental harm and, eventually, on the suicide rate, it is far too soon to know anything with certainty. But I doubt the news will be good. It is well known that the most common season for suicide is spring, when everything would appear to be returning to life, and the most popular day of the week for suicide is Monday, when people resume the effort of labour. So, the consequences of Covid-19 on suicide will not be felt until the situation significantly improves.

Indeed, there is evidence that situations like a pandemic, with self-isolation and lockdowns, are marginally better for people prone to depression. The thought here is that it is easier to deal with one's own depression when everyone else is miserable too. There is a solace in collective self-isolation for the melancholic temperament. Counting myself among their number, I must confess that I rather enjoyed lockdown, quarantine and the rest and am already rather nostalgic for its apparent austerities. In which case, it is the much-vaunted 'return to normal' that should be the cause for concern, the shared post-pandemic springtime. And we should be cognizant of the contagious effects of suicide, which are well-documented, and the fact that prevention efforts can also have the opposite effect of triggering the act. It is too soon to tell. As Larkin said of the reality of old age and decrepitude, we shall find out.

¶ I believe that some of the stigma surrounding mental illness has been diminished in the years since I wrote this essay – even professional football players are talking about depression these days. We are now perhaps more inclined to talk about suicide than we used to be. At least, I hope that this is the case. A large element of the motivation for writing this book was to widen the vocabulary around suicide, to find more words to describe and understand the phenomenon and treat it with empathy rather than empty platitudes.

What are we talking about when we talk about suicide? Something I repeatedly encountered, after I wrote this essay and was asked to talk about suicide, was a simple conceptual inadequacy. In many ways, the problem with suicide is that we stretch just one concept to fit across such a wide range of behaviours. The decision to end one's life in old age as a consequence of a terminal diagnosis and intolerable physical suffering is a very different matter from a sudden violent act in a moment of manic exuberance. The self-slaughter of a betrayed lover is very different from the carefully planned insanity of a suicide bomber. Suicide is a little like God. If someone asks me, 'Do you believe in God?', I'm always inclined to reply, 'Which one? There are so many.' At the very least, we need a range of more subtle and various concepts to describe the phenomena lumped together under the heading of suicide. In *The Noonday Demon*, Andrew Solomon has very helpfully begun this work by introducing four categories of suicide: (i) a manic, dire, impulsive and sudden act; (ii) revenge, or self-obliteration as payback for a felt wound; (iii) suicides which are planned, with complex and often lengthy notes, seemingly pragmatic but with a deeply faulty logic, 'as though they were organizing a holiday in outer space', as Solomon writes; and (iv) those planned through a reasonable logic, because of physical illness, mental instability or some catastrophic change in life's circumstances. To be clear, those people included under (iv) might be mistaken in their view, in particular the consequences that their action might have on their nearest and dearest, but we cannot say that they are deluded.

Solomon's categories are a beginning, it seems to me, but we would need to add more categories, such as the forms of suicide-homicide discussed in my essay, or the apparently inadvertent deaths that occur increasingly through fatal mixtures of drugs and alcohol, and where the question of intention is very hard to pin down. Such a list of categories could be extended. The important thing is for this work of reflection to continue and to move steadfastly away from any simple-minded idea of suicide as something which one must either be for or against, defend or oppose. It is infinitely more subtle than that. It is unclear whether suicide is unique to human beings. I have no difficulty in imagining an octopus killing itself. But there is nothing more human than suicide. Human beings are complex creatures. I see no reason why the discussion of the ways in which we sometimes choose to end our lives should be deprived of the same complexity.

Brooklyn, August 2020

'Shall we all die?
We shall die all.
All shall die we.
Die all we shall.'
Epitaph in Cunwallow Churchyard,
Cornwall, England

I.

This book is not a suicide note.

Ten days after Edouard Levé handed in the manuscript of *Suicide* to his publisher in 2007, he hanged himself in his apartment. He was 42. Two years after Jean Améry's *On Suicide* was published in 1976, the author took an overdose of sleeping pills. He was 65. In 1960, some eighteen years after Albert Camus had raised and – so he thought – resolved the question of suicide in *The Myth of Sisyphus*, he was killed in a car accident. He is alleged to have said that dying in a car crash is the most absurd of all deaths. The absurdity of his death is compounded by the fact he had an unused train ticket in his pocket. He was 46.

Let me say at the outset, at the risk of disappointing the reader, that I have no plans to kill myself... just yet. Nor do I wish to join the chorus of those who proclaim loudly against suicide and claim that the act of taking one's own life is irresponsible and selfish, even shameful and cowardly, that people must stay alive whatever the cost. Suicide, in my view, is neither a legal nor moral offence, and should not be seen as such. My intention here is to simply try to understand the phenomenon, the act itself, what precedes it and what follows. I'd like to consider suicide from the point of view of those who have made the leap, or have come close to it – we might even find that the capacity to take that leap is what picks us out as humans. I want to look at suicide closely, carefully, and perhaps a little coldly, without immediately leaping to judgements or asserting moral principles like the right to life or death. We have to look suicide in the face, long and hard, and see what features, what profile, what inherited character traits and wrinkles emerge. Perhaps what we see when we look closely is our own distorted reflection staring back at us.

Of course, regardless of his answer, Albert Camus' question in *The Myth of Sisyphus* is the right one. Judging whether life is worth living or not amounts to answering the fundamental philosophical question: should I live or die? To be or not to be? As we will soon see, the legal and *moral* framework that still shapes our thinking and judgement about suicide is hostage to a Christian metaphysics that declares that life is a gift of God. Therefore to take your own life is wrong, although Scripture nowhere explicitly forbids suicide (and, of course, Christ's crucifixion could be interpreted as a quasi-suicidal act). In killing oneself, it is claimed by Christian theologians, one is assuming a power over one's existence that only God should possess. Therefore, suicide is a sin.

From the nineteenth century onwards, this theological discourse was displaced by the rise of psychiatry, where suicide was not declared a sin but seen as a mental disorder requiring treatment of various kinds. This is still largely how we approach suicide: we speak readily (and not wrongly) of suicidal depression as an illness best approached through a combination of drugs – Lithium, say – and psychotherapy. But the implicit moral judgement on suicide that comes down to us from Christian theology remains intact and in force. Even when society or the state has taken the place of God, even when suicide is decriminalized, as it has been in the West for the past half century, it is still regarded as a kind of failing that invites an embarrassed response. We think that suicide is sad or wrong, often without knowing why. And we don't know what to say, other than mouth a few empty platitudes.

We lack a language for speaking honestly about suicide because we find the topic so hard to think about, at once both deeply unpleasant and gruesomely compelling. When someone ends their life, whether a friend, a family member or even a celebrity whom we identify with – think about the confused reactions to the deaths of Robin Williams and Philip Seymour Hoffman in recent times (although I suspect we could identify stories exerting a similar effect in any year) – one of two reactions habitually follow. We either quietly think that they were being foolish, selfish and irresponsible, or we decide that their actions were caused by factors outside of their control (severe depression, chronic addiction, and so on). That is, if they acted freely in killing themselves, we implicitly condemn them; but if we declare that their actions were constrained by uncontrollable behavioural factors like depression, we remove their freedom.

Against this tendency, I want to open up a space for thinking about suicide as a free act that should not be morally reproached or quietly condemned. Suicide needs to be understood and we desperately need a more grown-up, forgiving and reflective discussion of the topic. Too often, the entire debate about suicide is dominated by rage. The surviving spouses, families and friends of someone who committed suicide meet any attempt to discuss suicide with an understandable anger. But we have to dare. We have to speak.

Alongside the rage of the survivors, there is what appears to be a contradiction in our reaction to suicide. On the one hand, its horror silences us and we seem to find ourselves dumbfounded when a friend kills themselves. We might mutter, to no one in particular: 'How could he have done it?' 'What must his wife be going through? She just went out shopping, right?' 'Weren't the kids in the house at the time?' 'How exactly did he hang himself in his office?' But it is unclear, even as we run through these questions in our heads, why we are doing it. Are we looking for some explanation, some excuse, or perhaps some kind of relief that allows us to differentiate ourselves from the person who killed himself? Does it make us feel better? And if it does, should it?

Think about the following scenario, which happened to me not long ago in Paris. After dinner and some wine, an old friend of mine was telling me about the suicide of his close, childhood friend, whom I didn't know at all. I sat there and watched my friend tell the story of the suicide at length, and relate it to the suicides of other friends of his over the past several years. I could feel his rising emotion and it alarmed me. I knew that he had recently been suffering with depression. He was becoming visibly upset. I listened intently, not wanting to appear disrespectful or flippant. I really wanted to help, but found myself either asking dumb questions or uttering banalities, 'Well, at least he is at peace now.' It is as if our very proximity to suicide, the fact that our fate literally lies in our hands, is almost too much to bear, and words fail us. Our simultaneous nearness and distance from suicide silences us. Or we change the topic of conversation, 'So, what is Paul doing these days?'

On the other hand, the theme of suicide makes us singularly voluble. I am often asked socially, usually because people can think of nothing else to say, what I am working on, what I am writing. If I say, 'The relation between the sophist Gorgias and Euripidean tragedy' or 'The spatial technologies of memory' or 'Heidegger's conception of the completion of metaphysics and its overcoming', I am usually met with a polite 'Oh really? How interesting.' This is usually followed by an awkward pause. But if I say I am writing a little treatise on suicide then, after an initial hesitation, the floodgates open and a tide of fascinating stories, opinions and arguments flow forth. People begin to gush and recount stories of lives lost that could have been avoided. They speak of their friends' descent into the cold hell of depression, and maybe their own. They declaim happily about heroic and good deaths and – even more happily – about the inverse: the comically risible demise which invites a low, hollow laughter. They talk, often indirectly, of their own fear of death and the ways in which they have contemplated their end or perhaps even attempted to bring it about.

Suicide, then, finds us both strangely reticent and unusually loquacious: lost for words and full of them. But any contradiction is only apparent, not substantial. What we are facing here is an inhibition, a massive social, psychical and existential blockage that hems us in and stops us thinking. We are either desperately curious about the nasty, intimate, dirty details of the last seconds of a suicide and seek out salacious stories whenever we can. Or we can't look at all because the prospect is too frightening. Instead, we peek through the slits between our fingers with our hands on our face, as if we were watching a horror movie. Either way, we are hiding something, blocking something, concealing something through our silence or endless chatter or, indeed, rage.

¶ People don't throw their lives away lightly or willy -nilly. As David Hume said in his brilliant, short, posthumously published essay on suicide, 'I believe that no man ever threw away life, while it was worth keeping.' The clause that gives us pause is 'while it was worth keeping'. In what conditions is or is not life worth keeping? Hume's point is that when life has become a burden that cannot be borne, one is justified in taking it. The question is one of the limits of forbearance, which are limits that should be understood reflectively and with compassion using those two simple tools of empathy and introspection, which I borrow from Jean Améry.

At the risk of saying too much – and contradicting myself – there is something more than introspection at stake. For me, the question of suicide is not really or even remotely an academic issue. For reasons that we don't need to go into, my life has dissolved over the past year or so, like sugar in hot tea. For the first time in my life, I have found myself genuinely struggling with thoughts of suicide, 'suicidal ideation' as it is unhelpfully named. These thoughts take different forms, multiple fantasies of self-destruction, usually motivated by self-pity, self-loathing and revenge. I won't catalogue them. They are familiar, unsurprising and will emerge here and there obliquely as we proceed. Of course, to say this is to confess that the first sentence of this book is perhaps not to be trusted. But don't please be alarmed. As the character of Rust Cohle says in the HBO series *True Detective*, 'I lack the constitution for suicide.' Or again, in the words of the wonderful and much-missed English band, Black Box Recorder, 'Life is unfair: kill yourself or get over it.' This essay is an attempt to get over it.

After deciding to try and think through the question of suicide in the only way I know – in writing – I began to think about where to do it. I seemed to need some anchor, some mooring held tight and taut to the gravitational pull of the past, which would stop any drift and allow the words to come in a way that was unpressed, unfussed and unrushed. So, I have come here, to a pleasant and modestly sized coastal town in East Anglia: a place I visited on many occasions, not so far from where I lived until I moved to New York eleven years ago. I have rented a room in a hotel and have come to stare at the North Sea. Endless grey-green-brown waves are beating audibly against the beach as I write. The strand is pebbly underfoot and steeply banked. The wind is incessant and the rain unrelenting. Large gulls drift to and fro. Their calls disappear into gusts of air. A caravan of cumulus and cumulonimbus clouds endlessly tracks from west to east on their way to the Dutch coast, somewhere near Vlissingen, nominal source of New York's Flushing. The winter solstice approaches and the sun is a battered panache. The light flushes out of the year. I've come to meet the darkness in the darkness, at the end of the land, facing the sea: the vast, the unlimited.

Perhaps the closest we come to dying is through writing, in the sense that writing is a leave-taking from life, a temporary abandonment of the world and one's petty preoccupations in order to try to see things more clearly. In writing, one steps back and steps outside life in order to view it more dispassionately, both more distantly and more proximately. With a steadier eye. One can lay things to rest in writing: ghosts, hauntings, regrets, and the memories that flay us alive.

II.

Why is suicide seen as illegal, immoral or irreligious? The contrast between modern and ancient views of suicide is striking. Although Plato considered suicide a disgrace, he permitted notable exceptions, one of which allowed for self-killing by judicial order, as was the case with his teacher, Socrates. The practice of philosophy, then, begins with a suicide. To philosophize is to learn how to die, Socrates argues in the *Phaedo*, while at the same time telling his disciples stories of the immortality of the soul. Socrates was given the alternative of ostracism, which for him would have been even worse – the prospect of leaving Athens was worse than leaving life.

Faced with a more global and contingent imperial world, Stoics like Seneca took a more radical view of suicide, arguing that the brevity of human life was no source of woe. When a human life no longer flourishes because of bad fortune, one is permitted to end it. Seneca counsels that a wise person, a philosopher, 'lives as long as he ought, not as long as he can'. Famously, Seneca was ordered to kill himself by Nero, although his suicide was somewhat botched and it seems to have taken him an inordinate amount of time to expire. Tacitus reports that, being unable to die by bleeding because of advanced age and a frugal diet, Seneca asked for poison, like Socrates, but that also didn't work. Eventually, he was placed in a bath of hot water and suffocated to death by his servants.

Given this Greco-Roman background, what's the problem with suicide? How did our perception of suicide shift from its partial acceptance in antiquity to the prohibition on suicide that one can find in later centuries? The key to answering these questions is Christian theology. But I would like to approach the latter by way of a fascinating story about a little-known, indeed obscure, Italian philosopher called Count Alberto Radicati di Passerano e Cocconato (1698-1737). This will allow me to move through a series of arguments, positions and prejudices about suicide, almost in the manner of sweeping up debris, dead leaves and twigs, that might permit us to view the muddy ground beneath more clearly.

Born into an aristocratic family in Piedmont, Radicati converted to Protestantism and took up voluntary exile in London. In 1732, he published a 94-page pamphlet, *A Philosophical Dissertation upon Death*, where he sought to legitimize suicide against the moral and legal strictures of Christianity and the state. The pamphlet caused a huge stir in London and was declared by the Attorney General, at the repeated promptings of the Bishop of London, 'the most impious and immoral book'. Radicati was taken into custody, given a substantial fine and made his escape to the more tolerant United Provinces, the erstwhile name for the Netherlands. It is reported that, sadly, he died in complete destitution in Rotterdam some years later. He was attended by a Huguenot preacher who declared that, prior to his death, Radicati was filled with dread, renounced all he had written and was reconfirmed in the Protestant faith.

Radicati's simple thesis in his *Dissertation* is that individuals are free to choose their own death. This right to suicide was inspired by ancient arguments, notably from the Stoics, that suicide is a legitimate act and an honorable gesture of farewell from a state of unbearable pain, whether physical or psychical. Despite drawing on ancient thought, Radicati's views were so radical because they conflicted with Christian doctrine. Following a concept first formulated by Augustine and then refined by Thomas Aquinas, life, for the Christian, is something given – a *datum* – over which we have the right of use, *usus*, but not governance, *dominion*, which can only be the prerogative of God. To kill oneself is to exercise dominion over one's life and to assume the power that is only possessed by the deity. This is why suicide is a sin. A true Christian must battle with pain and fight on like a soldier.

The Christian view begins to break down in the seventeenth century with the rise of science and a materialist conception of nature. This builds from Thomas Hobbes's idea of reality as matter and motion and the atheistic interpretation of Spinoza, namely that when the latter begins the *Ethics* with the axiom 'God or Nature', what he really intends is material nature and nothing besides. According to this view, death is simply the dissolution of clusters of atoms, the transformation of one lump of matter into another. Radicati writes, 'We cease to exist in one sort, in order to exist in another.' Or, as Spinoza puts it, 'A free man thinks of nothing less than death, and his wisdom is a meditation on life, not on death.' In the demonstration of this proposition, Spinoza argues that a free human being is one who lives according to reason alone and is not governed by fear. To be free is to desire the good directly and to act and live in such a way as to persist in this desire without flinching or failing. This is why the free human being thinks of nothing less than death. Human life is simply an aspect of the vast, living vibrancy of a universe of matter. As Flaubert proposed a couple of centuries later, Spinoza's vision is extremely seductive, and it constitutes Saint Anthony's final and irresistible temptation: matter is God.

But if Radicati and Spinoza are right, then why do people fear death? This is where things start to get interesting. By definition, the fear of death cannot be based in experience as no one experiences death twice, as it were. Nor can the fear of death be ascribed to our natural, material constitution. Therefore, Radicati goes on, the fear of death has been imposed on humankind by, 'Ambitious Men, who, not contenting themselves with the State of Equality which Nature had given them, took it into their heads to thirst for Dominion over others.'

Who are these 'ambitious men'? Radicati is alluding to a book called the *Traité des trois imposteurs* (*Treatise of the Three Imposters*), also known as *L'Esprit de Spinosa* (*The Spirit of Spinoza*). Written in French and published anonymously in the Netherlands probably in the 1690s, the *Traité* is perhaps the most dangerous heretical text of the eighteenth century. It embodies the radical inheritance of the Enlightenment, evident in Spinoza and Hobbes – the tradition that came to be known as 'free-thinking'. (The great Irish philosopher John Toland, for example, was labelled a free-thinker by his idealist compatriot and relentless religious opponent, Bishop George Berkeley.) The *Traité* argues that Moses, Jesus and Mohammed are three imposters who have deceived humankind by imposing their 'silly ideas of God' and teaching 'the people to receive them without examination'. Central to this imposition is the cultivation of the fear of death, a belief that the three imposters propagate through the offices of their priestly castes.

Although Jesus nowhere condemns suicide and there is no explicit prohibition against suicide within the Mosaic Law of Judaism (although a Sura in the Qu'ran expressly forbids suicide), one gets the general picture. The fear of death is not natural to human beings, but instilled into them by the spurious authority of the Rabbi, the Priest or the Imam. What is fascinating in Radicati's text and the radical philosophical context that surrounds it is the connection between scientific materialism, anti-religious freethinking and the right to suicide.

But this was (and remains) no mere theoretical debate. In April 1732, shortly after the publication of Radicati's pamphlet, the shocking suicide of the Smith family was widely reported in England. Richard Smith and his wife, living in dreadful poverty in London, shot their daughter before hanging themselves. In his extended and carefully reasoned farewell letter, Smith, a book-binder by trade, makes allusion to Radicati's pamphlet. He writes that he and his family had decided to take leave of this friendless world rather than live in misery. They made this decision in complete cognizance of the laws prohibiting suicide, adding that it is 'indifferent to us where our bodies are laid'. The Smiths' (and one ineluctably thinks of Morrissey – heaven knows I'm mis-erable now) only wish was for an epitaph, which reads,

Without a name, for ever silent, dumb;
Dust, Ashes, Nought else is within this Tomb;
Where we were born or bred it matters not,
Who were our parents, or hath us begot;
We were, but now are not; think no more of us,
For as we are, so you be turned to Dust.

¶ Radicati's argument for the right to suicide was prefigured in an important treatise from 1644 by the great cleric and greater poet, John Donne. It was called *Biathanatos*, meaning literally 'death-force', or even the violence or strength of death. Donne's book bears a long and revealing subtitle: *A Declaration of that Paradox, or Thesis, that Self-Homicide is not so Naturally Sin, that it may*

39

never be Otherwise. Beginning from the fact that there is no condemnation of suicide in Scripture, Donne argues against the Christian doctrine that suicide is a natural sin and defends the right to 'self-homicide'. Fascinatingly, Donne confesses that 'a sickly inclination' compelled him to ponder the question of suicide, and when this sickness befell him, 'methinks I have the Keys of the Prison in mine own hand and no Remedy presents itself so soon to my Heart, as my sword'. The historian Silvia Berti notes that, by the time Donne's book was reissued in a second edition in 1700, it 'had become the manifesto of the free-thinker's right to die'.

The task of exposing the fallaciousness of Christian arguments against suicide begun by Donne and Radicati was completed with characteristic economy, aplomb and good humour by David Hume. He almost satirically un-picks Aquinas's position, which is based on the appeal to natural law enshrined in the alleged divine order of the cosmos. For example, Hume says, if the divine or-der means the causal laws created by God, then it must always be wrong to contravene such laws. But if that is the case, then *any* form of sickness, wounding or malady must not be treated since it is at odds with the laws of na-ture and divine will. Thus, the entire medical profession itself, insofar as it seeks to ameliorate the condition of the sick, should be outlawed. But that would be ridicu-lous, particularly as Christ was apparently rather fond of healing the sick and even, in the case of Lazarus, rais-ing the dead. Just as God permits us to divert water from rivers for the purpose of irrigation so too he ought to permit us to divert the blood from our veins. 'It would be no crime in me to divert the Nile or Danube from its course, were I able to effect such purposes. Where then is the crime of turning a few ounces of blood from their

40

natural channel?'

If suicide is a criminal act, Hume writes, then it must be a transgression of our duties either to God, our neighbour or our selves. It cannot be a transgression of any duty to God because of the spuriousness of the appeal to natural law. It would be a malevolent and wicked God that wished me to suffer unbearable, unceasing pain. As for my duties to myself, let's imagine that I am in a condition of great suffering from an incurable disease and my existence has become an intolerable burden to me. What possible duty could I have to myself to continue in such a state if the alternative is something I wish for? With regard to my neighbour and society, Hume writes that someone 'who retires from life, does no harm to society. He only ceases to do good; which, if it be an injury, is of the lowest kind.' On the contrary, Hume adds, we do no harm to ourselves or to others when existence has become a weight that is too heavy to carry. Suicide, he concludes, is 'the only way, that we can then be useful to society, by setting an example, which, if imitated, would preserve to every one his chance for happiness in life, and would effectively free him from all danger of misery'. The legitimacy of the recourse to suicide, namely the foreknowledge that I do not have to experience endless pain with either legal blame or moral shame, is the key to any chance for happiness. This is still a strong and highly relevant argument in relation to the debates on assisted or accompanied suicide. The wish of a terminally ill person is very often not so much happiness as death with dignity, without feeling they have acted illegally or immorally. Hume argues that suicide 'may be free from imputation of guilt and blame'.

What is most shocking about Hume's arguments is that they still have the capacity to shock, some 240 years after they were written. This is because the moral and legal framework in which suicide is viewed and judged is still tributary to the Christian doctrine that Hume so elegantly demolishes. Consider the definition of suicide in Sir William Blackstone's canonical *Commentaries on the Laws of England* (1765-69), which is a compiled record and interpretation of common law. Within the tradition of English common law, suicide was considered a felony and the equivalent of murder. Blackstone explains it in the following way, 'Felonious homicide is ... the killing of a human creature, of any age or sex, without justification or excuse ... this may be done by killing one's self, or another man.' Warming to its theme, the text continues,

> (T)he law of England wisely and religiously considers that no man hath a power to destroy life, but by commission from God, the author of it: and, as the suicide is guilty of a double offense; one spiritual, in invading the prerogative of the Almighty, and rushing into his immediate presence uncalled for; the other temporal, against the king, who hath an interest in the preservation of all his subjects; the law has therefore ranked this among the highest crimes, making it a peculiar species of felony, a felony committed on one's self... a *felo de se*.

With those words in mind, it might be recalled that Hamlet's first soliloquy expresses the vigorous wish to die, 'O, that this too too solid flesh would melt'. But he immediately restrains himself from the thought for it is criminal, 'that the Everlasting had not fix'd/ His canon 'gainst self-slaughter!' Canon law prohibits suicide.

In truth, suicide is a double crime: against God and against King (in Hamlet's case, this would be the imposter Claudius). Whoever takes their life is sinning against the eternal power of God and the temporal power of the King. To kill oneself is to usurp the sovereignty of God and King by assuming it for oneself. If one replaces the words 'God' or 'King' by 'state', 'society', 'country' or 'community', then it is clear that the situation hasn't really changed: rather than being seen as a free, sovereign act, suicide is seen as a usurpation of sovereignty, a morally embarrassing and reprehensible act of insubordination.

Of course, a rather obvious question arises: if suicide is a crime, then how can the perpetrator be punished? How does one discipline the dead? Once again, Blackstone provides the neat answer,

> [W]hat punishment can human laws inflict on one who has withdrawn himself from their reach? They can only act upon what he has left behind him, his reputation and fortune: on the former, by an ignominious burial in the highway, with a stake driven through his body; on the latter, by a forfeiture of all his goods and chattels to the king: hoping that his care for either his reputation, or the welfare of his family, would be some motive to restrain him from so desperate and wicked an act.

The French had even more stringent posthumous punishments for suicide. In 1670, Louis XIV declared a criminal ordinance for suicide, where it was decreed that the corpse must be drawn through the streets face down and then hanged or thrown on a garbage dump. Their property was also confiscated. The Sun King tolerated poorly the suicide of France's sons. In an English commentary on Chinese law from 1899, particular attention is paid to suicide pacts created for the profit of the surviving party. If it was proven that the parents entered into a suicide pact in order to aid the surviving child, then that child was to be decapitated.

Such punishments for the dead might seem either grisly or perhaps risible to us now, but it must be remembered that suicide is still a criminal offence in most Muslim countries. And, closer to home, although physician-assisted suicide became legal in Oregon in 1997, the great state of Missouri still classifies suicide as manslaughter (of course, the traditional, legal reasoning is perfectly logical: if someone else administers the fatal dose or lethal injection to the person who wants to die, then how can this qualify as self-killing?) Indeed, in New York State, although suicide is not considered a crime, it is still recognized by statute as a 'grave public wrong'. By implication, the deceased would be categorized as a grave public offender, even from their grave. Of course, the obvious and longstanding defence against suicide as a form of legal offense is to claim insanity, some form of diminished responsibility or to not be, in the words of Blackstone, 'in one's senses'.

It's clear that the Christian prohibition against suicide continues to shape our moral thinking, often unknowingly and subtly. If suicide is a free act, made 'in one's senses', then it is an offense to God, King and country; if suicide is adjudged to have taken place with diminished responsibility or some form of mental illness like severe depression, then freedom is eliminated. Either way, the moral, philosophical and existential space for the consideration of suicide as a free act is closed down. It is this space that I would like to explore.

¶ It is sometimes said that suicide is wrong because only God has proper moral authority over our lives. We are God's property, as it were. But if so, humans are queer or weird property because we still somehow have the impression of acting under our own volition. People are not pot plants sitting passively in some divine greenhouse. However the capacity for free will is understood, it permits us to act against divine will. Although I might wish to align my imperfect will with the perfect will of God in order to act well, such alignment is, and moreover must, never be attained. If I claim that my will is God's will, then I am implicitly claiming that all my actions are divinely sanctioned, which is hubristic, if not sinful. Within the Christian tradition, I might incline my will towards God in an act of faith in the hope of receiving grace, but grace is never something I can bestow on my self or my actions. To be human is to be able to act contrary to God's will. If we are God's property, then we were created with the capacity to act improperly. Such is the lesson of the Fall and expulsion east from Eden.

Another religious argument is that suicide is prohibited because life is a gift from God. To kill oneself is to refuse that gift. But this becomes muddled if one thinks about it for a moment: if life is a gift from God, then what exactly is a gift? A gift is something one gives to another person. After the act of giving, the gift belongs to its recipient. By definition, the giver of the gift no longer has possession of the gift once it is given. So, if the prohibition against suicide is based on the idea that life is a gift from God, then life appears to be a gift with many strings attached, which entails that it is no longer a gift. Namely, a gift that we cannot reject is not a gift. In order to be a gift, life has to be capable of being refused, thrown away, re-gifted to someone else, re-sold for money or given away. If life is a gift from God, then God must allow for the possibility of suicide as the rejection of that gift. On the basis of this argument, suicide cannot be condemned.

The same objection works against secular versions of this position, which are not uncommon. If one says that suicide is wrong because of the belief that life is a gift, not from God, but from one's parents, one's community, or one's place in some more numinous natural or cosmic order, then this argument is also muddled. If life is a gift from one's parents, say, then in order to be a gift it has to be received along with the possibility of being refused, otherwise it is the attempted sheer imposition of will. Whatever bond or generational contract exists between parents and children, this must not exclude *a priori* the possibility of the suicide of one's child, as profoundly painful and deeply troubling as that must be (I can imagine nothing worse). If life is a gift, then it is given to its recipient with no strings attached.

It is sometimes said – in fact, it is quite often said – that God is all-loving. Let's imagine that this is the case. But if God is all-loving, then should not such love extend to permitting the suicide of one of his creatures when their suffering has become too hard to bear? How could an all-loving God demand the continuation of intolerable suffering? To demand such continuation would be to confuse love with the sheer force of a commandment. God would be saying, 'I forbid you to take your life.' But that is not love. After all, what is love? I think Oscar Wilde is right when he defines love in *De Profundis* as giving what one does have and receiving that over which one has no power. To love is to commit oneself to another not without the guarantee that love will be returned, but with the hope that it might be. Love takes place in the subjunctive mood: it may be, it might be, would that it were the case. The logic of love is akin to the logic of grace. I give something that is truly beyond my capacity to control, I commit myself to it completely, but there can be no assurance that love will be reciprocated. At any point in a love relation, the beloved can and must be able to say 'I love you not.' If this is not the case, if the beloved cannot refuse love, then love is reduced to coercive control, to contractual obligation and command. None of these is love. If God is all-loving, then he, she or it has to allow us to refuse that love and take our life and death into our own hands.

Christian arguments against suicide turn on the extension of the sixth commandment 'thou shalt not kill' to the questionable interpretation that this commandment forbids self-killing as well. I do not see the entailment between forbidding the murder of others – a wholly legitimate aspiration – to the prohibition of suicide, which is premised on a misunderstanding of the nature of human liberty. In addition, the prohibition of self-killing poses a huge problem in the interpretation of cases of martyrdom and the deaths of innumerable saints, particularly when one considers the early history of Christianity. The Christian martyrs chose to go to their deaths out of love of God and hatred of the state or any other form of temporal, pagan authority. If the crucifixion of Christ himself can be viewed as a quasi-suicidal act performed out of love, then this is *a fortiori* the case with the deaths of saints and martyrs who imitate Christ's sacrifice. It would seem to be completely contradictory to forbid suicide while celebrating the quasi-suicidal acts of the saints. The martyr is a witness who testifies to his or her deep love of God *all* the way to giving up their life because of that love. But the act of martyrdom, like witness itself, has to be a free act chosen out of love, otherwise the saints are simply God's puppets or robots. What we admire in the deaths of the saints is their freely chosen capacity to act out of faith in a way that overrides their self-interest and selfishness. But their example cannot provide the basis for an absolute prohibition of suicide. On the contrary: in order for there to be a world where saintliness is possible, then we have to allow for the precariousness of human freedom. Otherwise, God's love collapses into tyranny.

Related confusions can be found in the idea of the sanctity of life. One hears this a great deal. Someone might say: 'I object to suicide because I believe in the sanctity of life, and killing oneself is a violent and illegitimate denial of life's sacredness.' But what is the implication of this belief? If life is sacred, then it is not the case that only suicide is prohibited: all forms of killing are forbidden. A belief in the sanctity of life entails, for a start, an opposition to capital punishment. To believe that suicide is a crime because life is sacred while also believing in the death penalty (there are many Americans who appear to hold both beliefs) is a sheer contradiction. Similarly, if life is sacred, then all forms of killing are forbidden, for example during wartime. To follow through the logic of the argument for the sanctity of life would also forbid killing in self-defence. What possible justification could there be for killing another person – an attacker, a burglar, a rapist, a junky *with* a knife – in self-defence if I believe that life is sacred? In order to be consistent, a belief in the sanctity of life has to lead to a complete quietism and utter pacifism (some religious groups, such as The Society of Friends or the

Quakers, have nobly tried to live and practice their faith in accordance with such pacifism). Also, if life is sacred, then all life is sacred, and it is also forbidden to take the lives of cows, sheep, chicken or fish in order to feed oneself. And why stop there? What about cockles, mussels and crustaceans (remember, I am writing overlooking the North Sea)? And are not fruit and vegetables also alive? What about wheat, barley and grass? A belief in the sanctity of life demands a saintliness of which not even Saint Francis was capable, let alone his eponymous successor in the Vatican.

To tell the truth, the inner lining of a belief in the sanctity of life is pretty ragged, ugly-looking and intolerant. If life possesses intrinsic value – and, for the purposes of argument, let's restrict this to human life – then this entails that all forms of life possess such value and it is not permitted in any circumstances to take a human life. This means that it is not permitted to end the life of someone who is in a permanently vegetative state, either as a consequence of an illness or perhaps due to a serious stroke. One must, in all circumstances, keep the person alive, however awful and intense their suffering, however pointless their life might have become, however they might have wished to end their life with dignity. For example, think of someone who has made an explicit agreement with their spouse or family that their life should be ended once they enter a permanently vegetative state. But let's also imagine that they live within a jurisdiction – and this is not at all uncommon, especially in the United States – where it is forbidden to end the life of a patient because that state believes in the sanctity of life. In such a case, the person's life must be pointlessly extended and their freely chosen wishes simply ignored. How can that be right?

¶ Religious arguments around the prohibition of suicide quickly become confused. But, sadly or happily (depending on one's point of view) non-religious arguments become equally muddled.

It might sound to the reader as if I am making a straightforwardly libertarian anti-religious argument about suicide, namely that I should be free to choose the time, space and means of my death when I wish. This position perhaps has something to recommend it, but sadly it is also flawed. If I claim that I have the right to suicide, the right to decide about my own death, then the major premise of this claim is that I enjoy complete self-possession, self-ownership or sovereignty over myself. It conceives of the relation to my self in analogy with the relation to my possessions, like a computer or a fridge. But do I enjoy self-ownership in the same manner in which I own a fridge? Not at all. Whatever my 'self' might be, it is something that is partially my own, but also partially shared with others, either those who formed me without my choosing them, like my parents, siblings and sadistic elementary school teachers, or those whom I choose to share my life with, like my friends and comrades, and those whom I love, like my spouse and children.

It is something of a banality to say that we are relational beings, but that doesn't stop it being true. If the right to suicide flows from some idea of self-ownership, then I would be inclined to say that we do not own ourselves. It is not that we are completely owned by others, but self-possession is something possessed with others, alongside them. Life is not lived in some lofty independence. We are dependent rational creatures and such dependency is not a limitation of my freedom. It is its condition. Think back to my fridge. To what extent is it mine? I might have paid for it, but it is something I share with the people I live with: family, guests, visitors and subletters. My computer might feel like it's mine, but the machine on which I am writing is marked on the underside with a prison-like serial number and an indelible sticker proclaiming 'Property of The New School'.

The problem with any claim to the right to suicide based on self-ownership is that it is simply the dialectical inversion of the claims to sovereignty that we saw above in the quotations from Blackstone's commentaries on common law. If I choose to rebel against the idea that suicide is prohibited because it is a double crime against the sovereignty of God and King, then that does not entail that I am sovereign over myself. If I choose to refuse God and King, then that does not entail that I am my own God or King, like crazy Robinson Crusoe driven to psychotic delusions on his desert island. Such is the lie of all forms of possessive individualism. Sovereignty is something shared and divided in the complex networks of dependency that constitute a human life. In relation to the question of suicide, claims to sovereignty very quickly become murky.

Something similar flows from the claim that the right to suicide is the natural corollary to the inalienable right to life. But this is also murky. Does it follow from the fact that no one – God, King or state – is permitted to kill me that I am permitted to kill myself? If the right to life is inalienable, then how can I alienate myself from life through a suicidal act? A moment's thought reveals the strangeness, if not absurdity, of the two-step logic to which I would then be committed. If I believe in the inalienable right to life, then I must somehow alienate myself from that right in order to then kill myself. First I must renounce the right to life and then I must kill myself. But what is the justification for the second step? It cannot be the right to life, as that has already been renounced. Is it necessary to invoke some second right: a right to death, perhaps? Or I could just admit that the right to life is indeed alienable? But what then would grant me the right to alienate myself from that right? Wouldn't it be equally justified for God, King or the state to claim that they too possessed the right to alienate me from my right to life? In which case, we are back where we started with the theological prohibition of suicide, except in a state of even deeper confusion.

¶ This leads to the provisional conclusion that perhaps all talk of rights in relation to suicide is doomed to severe conceptual confusion, whether that right is deemed to be exerted by God, King, the sovereign state or the sovereign self. At this point, it might be helpful to turn from the language of rights to that of duties, but sadly the arguments here are equally confused and confusing. Do our duties to others override our personal claim to the 'right' to suicide? In other words, is suicide selfish? Suicide can and does cause immense grief to those we love and are close to and may also have significant effects on those further away. (On 12 August, 2014, the day after the suicide of Robin Williams, calls to the suicide hotline in the US doubled from a typical 3,500 per day to about 7,400.) Suicide can cause considerable emotional harm on one's loved ones, as well as material harm, in the form of economic effects. This is undeniable, but it does not constitute an argument for an absolute prohibition of suicide. Questions of the harm to others have to be balanced against the harm that would be caused by forcing the suicidal person to continue to live in a situation of unendurable physical or psychical suffering. Should Robin Williams, who obviously endured intense depression, have been obliged to live for the sake of his family or his fans? I am dubious as to whether we can make that judgment with moral certainty.

There is also much talk about 'community' and one's duties to it in relation to suicide. But this is also muddy. Firstly, it is unclear what kind of 'communities' most of us live in at this point in the early twenty-first century, and what kinds of bonds bind us to them, imaginary or ideological, felt or real. At least the talk of God and King has more metaphysical substance than the largely wishful thinking about 'community'. Secondly, what kind of 'community' is it that forces its members to stay alive when they don't want to? Most people don't choose where they were born or where they live. What kind of duty does one have to something that one didn't choose? And if one is fortunate enough to choose to live in another 'community', then what duties does one have towards it? Even if one chooses to live in a certain 'community', does that necessarily remove the choice to end one's life? And if there exists (which I very much doubt) some kind of tacit or explicit 'social contract', then what kind of contract is it that does not have an opt-out clause, particularly when most of us didn't choose to opt-in in the first place?

Consider the inverse of this position. If I have a duty to society or the 'community' not to kill myself, then doesn't society have a reciprocal duty not to kill me or threaten me with death, either in the form of capital punishment or through military conscription, where I might die in a theatre of war or a terrorist attack? As we saw with the argument for the sanctity of life, it seems to me that the only kind of 'community' that might be able to demand a duty of not killing oneself is a complete and thoroughgoing pacifist society. As lovely as the prospect of such a society might be, it is unclear whether it has ever existed or is indeed likely to exist.

Now, consider the perverse version of this inversion with the example of the brilliant 2006 movie *Children of Men*, directed by Alfonso Cuarón and based on the 1992 novel by P. D. James. The movie depicts a world, not unlike our own, where increasingly anxious, authoritarian regimes are obsessed with homeland security and where the business of politics is based on a cocktail of atavistic nationalism and a terror of immigration and immigrants. At its core the story in *Children of Men* revolves around the fact that human beings have ceased to be able to reproduce and face the imminent prospect of extinction. Britain sees itself as the last country in the world to maintain any semblance of order and its crypto-fascist government has issued a drug called (with a nod to *Hamlet*) 'Quietus'. Citizens are encouraged to take their own lives for the benefit of the greater good. I think this scenario shows the problem with all arguments against suicide based on a duty to the 'community'. But in the case of *Children of Men* a citizen's duty consists in taking their own life for the good of the 'community'. It is not at all inconceivable, to my mind, to picture a slippery slope from a legal and moral position where suicide is permitted, whether assisted, accompanied or not, to one where society exerts a gentle or not so gentle force on those people it considers useless, surplus to requirements or free-riders to kill themselves: 'Go on, do the right thing by the community and kill yourself. At least someone may get your job and there will be one less mouth to feed.'

¶ In the name of ground-clearing, I hope to have shown that the arguments both for and against suicide based on conceptions of rights or duties begin to fall apart when gently pressed and prodded. The familiar claims and counterclaims about suicide tend to dissolve into a sea mist that evaporates into the air with the turning tide.

What about the claim that suicide is justified if it is rationally chosen? What if I spent the next few days calmly and rationally weighing the arguments pro and con as to whether I should kill myself? Let's say that I came to the conclusion, on the reasonable balance of evidence, that I should end it all now. I could even write these reasons down in form of a suicide note and leave it in an envelope on my hotel bed and disappear into the engulfing, ever-churning sea.

But how can the decision to end one's life ever be rational? In order for it to be rational, I would have to look at the reasons for being alive and assess them against the reasons for being dead. But as being dead is not something I have exactly experienced, how can I make a rational assessment of that state as being preferable to my current situation? The truth is that I obviously cannot. At which point, one is inclined to cite the sagacious Epicurus: when death is, I am not; when I am, death is not; therefore why worry? Epicurean wisdom was intended to be a cure for the fear of death by removing the longing for immortality. But the point is that the justification for suicide on the basis of rationality has to confront the fact that reason cannot peer into death and make any rational assessment. Dead man don't do discourse.

The same line of argument could be extended to the claim that I am justified in taking my life because it is an autonomous decision. For some philosophers, like Kant, rationality and autonomy are two sides of the same moral coin. The only law to which I am legitimately subject is one that I legislate for myself. But how can I be autonomous in relation to suicide? Am I not making an autonomous decision to rid myself of autonomy? How can autonomy be consistent with a definitive decision to abandon it? Is not the very fact of death heteronomous, a giving myself over to something outside of my control, some range of experience that I can never experience, namely death? Is not suicide therefore implicitly irrational? Is it not a leap into the dark? A leap of faith?

The claim that suicide is an irrational leap of faith might seem to provide transient comfort. But it shouldn't. I am reminded of a terrifying moment in Maurice Blanchot's novel *Thomas the Obscure* that has stayed with me since I first read the book three decades ago. Blanchot writes,

> Just as the man who is hanging himself, after kicking away the stool on which he stood, heading for the final shore, rather than feeling the leap which he is making into the void feels only the rope which holds him, held to the end, held more than ever, bound as he had never been before to the existence he would like to leave.

The awful prospect that Blanchot so powerfully describes is that all the suicidal person experiences after the leap into the dark is the rope that ties them ever more tightly to the existence they wanted to leave. The suicide experiences themselves bound as never before to the existence they rationally or irrationally wanted to leave behind. If suicide is an irrational leap, then why on earth should we rationally take it?

Isn't the perhaps conquerable fear of death always

outweighed by the terror of *dying*? Maybe the experience of dying will be infinitely worse than the alternative, namely to stay and endure. Maybe that is the truth of Epicurean wisdom: as you know nothing of death, you should do nothing to bring it about: *live instead*. I am reminded of Dorothy Parker's famous lines on the comparative merits of various methods of dispatch:

Razors pain you
Rivers are damp
Acids stain you
And drugs cause cramp.
Guns aren't lawful
Ropes tend to give
Gas smells awful
You might as well live.

Parker attempted suicide at least five times before succeeding with an overdose of barbiturates in 1967. Her final note read, 'Any royalties on my books are to go to John McClain, my clothes and my wristwatch to my sister, Helen Droste, and also my little dog, Robinson.' What is so poignant here is the precise attention to detail: the wristwatch, the little Crusoe-like dog.

The question of rationality with respect to suicide is severely complicated by the fact that would be self-killers often plan their demises with a meticulous precision that seems utterly reasonable to them at the time. Rationality is usually combined with severe depression, which causes havoc with one's reason. I think for example of the suicide of the Japanese writer Yukio Mishima with a ritual hara-kiri, which he administered to himself, after shouting, 'Long live the Emperor!', with a deep 17 cm (nearly 7 inches) incision into his abdomen. Sadly, the suicide was botched and one of Mishima's soldiers had to administer the final blow, but he missed, twice. The third blow was on target, but not strong enough. Another soldier had to finish the task with a decapitation. At which point, the room had begun to smell as Mishima's intestines were lying on the ground. Mishima believed with consummate rationality that his suicide could save Japanese honour in a dishonourable world. Whether it is dreams of martyrdom, delusions of paradise or fantasies of honour and revenge, there is a perverse rationality to depressive suicide where all reasons lead to the same fatal and seemingly inescapable decision. Reason runs headlong into one last, long tunnel with no exit.

Truly, one has to be inside such a mental state in order to fully understand it. I defer here to the testimony of Kay Redfield Jamison, a clinical psychologist and author of *An Unquiet Mind*. She gives an extremely humane and informed personal account of suicidal depression, through to her recovery through a careful combination of psychotherapy and drug therapy. She writes that 'Suicidal depression is a state of cold, agitated horror and relentless despair. The things you most love in life leach away. Everything is an effort, all day and throughout the night. There is no hope, no point, no nothing.'

In an attempt to understand suicide and the fatal logic of its tunnel vision, I'd like to turn to the most compelling form of evidence that we possess: the suicide note.

III.

In May 2013, I organized a suicide note creative writing workshop. It was part of a two-week art installation, in a tiny space on Manhattan's West 21st Street, called 'The School of Death', that I curated with my friend, Sina Najafi. The pop-up school came about as a rather sly and admittedly smart-alecky reaction to something called The School of Life in London, which retails a rather nauseating philosophy of self-help to the English upper-middle classes in search of some vague notion of enlightenment. It was also intended as a way of poking a stick into the ever-growing ash pile of creative writing classes.

Despite the time of year, it was chilly and it rained constantly on the Saturday afternoon I was scheduled to run the class as a way of closing the show and putting an end to The School of Death. To my surprise, fifteen or so people turned up, along with a journalist from the *New York Times*, who lurked awkwardly in the doorway. The glass doors of the small space were open in order to allow for people to spread out. Everyone was huddled in coats and jackets against the cold and we sat on the floor.

One always speaks to someone in a suicide note. Suicide notes are attempts at communication. They are a last and usually desperate attempt to communicate – final communications. They are also failed attempts in the sense that the writer is communicating a failure to communicate, expressing the desire to give up in one last attempt at expression. The suicidal person does not want to die alone, but wants to die with another or others, to whom the note is addressed.

The suicide note might have existed in antiquity, perhaps even as far back as ancient Egypt. It rose to prominence in its recognizable, modern form in the eighteenth century in England as a consequence of literacy and the rapid rise and spread of newspapers. The peculiar thing about eighteenth-century suicide notes is the fact that they were routinely sent to the press by those intending to take their lives, as we saw with the Smith family's last words. The modern suicide note is in origin, then, a publication, an intensely public act, a perverse piece of publicity. The historical evidence might give us pause when we shroud the suicide note in secrecy, as we now tend to do, and consider it the sacrosanct domain of the spouse or family. Sometimes it is, but often it is not.

Indeed, the desire to keep the details of suicide secret is questionable. As everyone knows, the Golden Gate Bridge is a popular suicide destination. Yet all the suicides jump from the side of the bridge that faces San Francisco. No one wants to jump from the side that faces out to the Pacific Ocean. Peculiar, no? It is, unless one accepts that suicide is very often a public act, an act of publicity. This perhaps begins to explain the popularity of certain suicide locations, like the Brooklyn Bridge, Beachy Head on the south coast of England, Toronto's Bloor Street Viaduct, or the now heavily secured and fenced-in bridges that span the gorges of Cornell University in upstate New York, a popular Ivy League suicide spot.

The suicide note, then, is a form of display, the symptom of a deliberate exhibitionism. True, for their readers, suicide notes are a kind of pornography. We are allowed to become voyeurs into a hidden or forbidden state of mind and the notes exercise a kind of sick attraction. But that doesn't mean we shouldn't look. We might learn something. It is also arguable that the exhibitionism of the suicide note is a characteristic of the melancholic or depressed person. The odd thing about melancholics – which, lest we forget, includes very many of us – is that they don't keep quiet, but tend to proclaim endlessly and volubly about their misery.

Of course, the paradigm case here is the suicidal Hamlet, who is not just content to feel profound grief at the murder of his father and the hurried remarriage of his mother to his father's murderer, but who tells us about it in soliloquy after soliloquy. What is most striking about Hamlet's speeches is not their delusional quality, but their perspicacity. What he complains about – the nature of grief, the futility of war, the illusory power of theatre, the obscurity of our parents' desire (especially our mother's) and most of all his doubts about the nature of existence – is powerfully true. The ceaseless self-accusations of the melancholic are very often accurate. What we see in Hamlet is a powerful cocktail of depression and exhibitionism.

¶ Freud gives us the recipe for this cocktail with chilling clarity in his brilliant paper, 'Mourning and Melancholia', from 1917. If mourning is the grief that we feel in response to the death of someone beloved that leads us to lament and plaint, then in melancholia the object of this grief is no longer the dead beloved, but ourselves. What happens in depression, for Freud, is that the self turns against itself, the subject makes itself into an object, and complains bitterly. 'Why, what an ass am I!' as Hamlet says. In depression, the self sees itself ass-backwards, as it were, and finds itself horribly wanting and deficient. The self's sadistic urges flip over into a lacerating masochism, where we ceaselessly berate ourselves for our faults. In Freud's terms, the ego's narcissistic self-love becomes the basis for self-hatred.

For Freud, this is the solution to the riddle of suicide, which makes melancholia so fascinating (for we *are* compelled by Hamlet's endless, staged antics) and so dangerous. The argument here has two important steps. First, Freud writes,

> So intense is the ego's self-love, which we have come to recognize as the primal state from which instinctual life proceeds, and so vast is the amount of narcissistic libido which we see liberated in the fear that emerges at a threat to life, that we cannot conceive how the ego can consent to its own destruction.

As Freud writes elsewhere, hate is older than love. The primal constitution of the self takes place in a narcissistic libido that seeks self-preservation at all costs. But if that is true, then how is suicide possible? This requires a second step:

> The analysis of melancholy now shows that the ego can kill itself only if, owing to the return of object-cathexis, it can treat itself as an object – if it is able to direct against itself the hostility which relates to an object and which represents the ego's original reaction to objects in the external world.

Freud's point, besides the mumbo-jumbo about 'object-cathexis', is crystal clear: given our intense self-love, in order to kill ourselves we have to turn ourselves into objects. More precisely, we have to turn ourselves into objects that we hate. Thus, suicide is strictly speaking impossible. I cannot kill *myself*. What I kill is the hated

64

object that I have become. I hate that thing that I am and I want it to die. Suicide is homicide.

It is this idea of suicide as homicide that David Foster Wallace describes with great precision and pathos in the extraordinary commencement speech given at Kenyon College in 2005, *This is Water*. He admits that it is a banality to say that the mind is a great servant but a terrible master. But nonetheless, it is true. And this is the reason why, he adds, people who commit suicide with firearms shoot themselves in the head rather than the heart. They want to kill that terrible master. This is Freud's point. Suicide is the determination to rid ourselves of what enslaves us: the mind, the head, the brain, that vague area of febrile activity somewhere behind our eyes.

This also partially explains the phenomenon of the suicide note and its mixture of depression and exhibitionism, where self-love becomes hatred and one dies apologizing for one's actions. Before drowning himself in the River Seine, the poet Paul Celan underlined the following line from a biography, 'Sometimes this genius goes dark and sinks down into the bitter well of his heart.' Through writing the suicide note, one turns oneself into an object, an object that is hated and must be drowned in a bitter well. A 50-year-old Massachusetts man wrote,

I'm done with life
I'm no good
I'm dead.

But there is a further twist to the dialectic of the suicide note. The hatred that permits us to overcome our self-love and kill ourselves is also the occasion for the most extreme exclamations of love. It is as though the intensity of self-hatred allows a final, heartfelt and equally intense proclamation of love. These twinned energies of love and hate dramatically pull apart, and we fall into the abyss that opens up beneath us.

The suicide note is the stage where the profound ambivalence of love and hate plays itself out. Kurt Cobain wrote more than one suicide note. On letter paper from a hotel in Rome in March 1994, he wrote 'Like Hamlet, I have to choose between life and death. I choose death.' Cobain's final note, from 5 April 1994, is powerfully revealing. He begins by expressing a yearning for the loving innocence of childhood, 'I'm too sensitive. I need to be slightly numb in order to regain the enthusiasm I had as a child.' The ambivalence then swings around before swinging back:

> Since the age of seven, I've become hateful toward all humans in general ... I'm too much of an erratic, moody baby! I don't have the passion anymore, and so remember, it's better to burn out than to fade away. Peace, love and empathy, Kurt Cobain.

At the foot of the page, Cobain writes in huge capital letters: 'I LOVE YOU! I LOVE YOU!' When Courtney Love read out Cobain's note at his funeral, she finished by saying to the crowd, 'Just tell him he's a fucker, OK? ... And that you love him.' The ambivalence of Cobain's suicide note of love and hate is captured precisely in Love's hate. This is what Jacques Lacan called '*hain-amoration*', 'hate-love'.

One of the most poignant suicide notes I know is simply,

Dear Betty:
I hate you.
Love,
George.

We die hating the one we loved and wanting to punish them with our death: 'There, see how you feel now. I bet you're gonna love me now I'm no longer there. I bet you regret what you did now, don't you? Huh?'

¶ The ambivalence of love and hate finds expression in suicide as a form of revenge, as retribution for a perceived injustice, a felt wrong. Euripides's heroine Medea does not kill herself, but kills her two sons out of revenge for the wrong done to her by her husband, Jason. There are many modern Medeas, not all of them women. In 2014, in Secunderabad in India, Dr Aluru Raghavendra Guruprasad, an assistant professor from a private business school with more than thirty authored or co-authored scientific publications, killed his two sons before throwing himself in front of a train. He was apparently angry with his former wife for not being allowed to spend enough time with his sons. And this evening in East Anglia on the local news, as I write these words, it was reported from Lowestoft, Suffolk, that a 35-year-old woman had killed her three children, placing their corpses in their beds, each daubed in lipstick with the words 'I love you.' She then drowned herself in the sea, the same cold North Sea I am looking at now.

The phenomenon of revenge suicide can escalate into more political forms of self-killing. Before killing three Israeli soldiers on a suicide mission, Hisham H wrote, 'The life of this world is just a game and accumulation of possessions and children. What God has is better for me than this.' In protest against the war in Vietnam, a teacher in Saigon immolated herself in front of a pagoda with pictures of the Virgin Mary and the Buddhist goddess of mercy by her side. Her note said the following:

MY INTENTION
I wish to use my body as a torch
To dissipate the darkness
To waken love among men
And to bring Peace to Vietnam.

On 17 December 2010, Mohamed Bouazizi, a street vendor from Tunisia, immolated himself because of police harassment and ignited the conflagration that some called the Arab Spring. He died from his injuries on 4 January 2011. We might think of these as cases of 'altruistic suicide', where one kills oneself in order to bring attention to a perceived injustice, such as the self-immolation of Tibetan monks, like Thupten Ngodup in 1998, in protest against the Chinese occupation of their country.

Other surface motives appear in suicide notes. In his will Adolf Hitler declared that 'My wife and I choose to die in order to escape the shame of overthrow and capitulation,' (although I wonder if this might not be a case of Adolf turning to Eva Braun and saying, 'I'm going to kill myself, aren't we?'). During the Nuremberg Trials after the Second World War, Herman Göring, founder of the Gestapo and *Reichsmarschall* of Germany, poisoned himself out of pride when he heard that the Allies were going to hang him rather than shoot him. In Göring's worldview, being shot would have been a more noble and fitting exit for a man of his considerable stature.

Suicide can also appear to be a business decision. Alex C battled the Inland Revenue Service (IRS) for years at enormous cost. He explained his suicide to his wife in the following terms:

> I have taken my life in order to provide capital for you. The IRS and its liens which have been taken against our property illegally by a runaway agency of our government have dried up all sources of credit for us. So I have made the only decision I can. It's purely a business decision. I hope you can understand that. I love you completely...

Note here both the conviction that no other decision is possible and the declaration of complete love. Alex C's hope was that his wife would receive the insurance money after his death. With unintended bathos, his note ends with the words, 'You will find my body on the lot on the north side of the house.' Since the financial crisis of 2008, examples of such suicides are all too common. Research suggests a strong correlation between unemployment and suicide, with studies showing that the suicide rate amongst the unemployed has risen significantly since the 1990s. In response to a story published in the *New York Times* on 2 May 2013, about a sharp rise in suicide rates in the US, Jen D from New Jersey wrote:

> Economic hopelessness. My brother committed suicide last July. He had just turned 60. He lost his IT job in the Great Recession in 2008. Despite hundreds of resumes being sent out, and a lifetime of IT experience, he got few interviews and no job offers. He spent down his 401(k) and when he died the only thing he owned was a beat-up car. We later found out he had a lot of credit card debt,

with which he had tried to keep himself afloat. After four years of no job offers, unemployment running out, having no health insurance, etc., his dignity was shot. He had lost hope of ever working again. How I wish he had not committed suicide; how I would give anything and everything to have him back. I consider him one of the casualties of the Recession and when I read of the fat bonuses the banksters award themselves, I shake with rage that they have continued to prosper while people like my brother lost all hope and people like me lost a loved one.

Such testimony surpasses commentary.

¶ Behind the apparent motives of shame, pride or a simple business decision, there lies the deeper sense of suicide as a righteous act of recrimination against a perceived injustice that necessitates the act of taking one's life. Many of the examples of suicide notes already cited converge on the idea that there can be no alternative to suicide, other than to suffer further humiliation. Once taken, the decision seems irrevocable.

In extreme cases, such righteous acts of suicide often merge with fantasies of victimization to devastating effect. The most infamous of these is the mass suicide of Jim Jones and the People's Temple in Guyana on 18 November 1978, when 918 people died, including 276 children. The children were forced to drink grape-flavoured Kool-Aid laced with cyanide before their parents did the same. While hundreds of people were dying, Jim Jones gave a long sermon, to the bizarre accompaniment of organ music. His persecutory fantasy was that the US government was going to destroy him and all his followers in reprisal for their murder of Leo Ryan, a US

Congressman, who had tried to visit their community on a government fact-finding mission. Jones declaims,

> If we can't live in peace then let's die in peace ... we are not committing suicide – it's a revolutionary act ... this is a revolutionary suicide council. I'm not talking about self – self-destruction, I'm talking about that we have no other road.

After exhorting the children to drink the poisoned Kool-Aid and to remain calm — 'Children, it will not hurt' — he concludes,

> We used to think that this world was not our home, and it sure isn't ... take our life from us. We laid it down, we got tired. We didn't commit suicide, we committed an act of revolutionary suicide protesting the conditions of an inhumane world.

All the while, the organ music grinds on.

What is so striking in the example of Jonestown is the complete disavowal of any responsibility for the act of mass death and the certainty that there is no other option. Once the decision is taken, always against one's will, there can be no other path of action. One delivers oneself up into the hands of Fate.

It is in terms of the suicide note as a persecutory fantasy of victimization and complete disavowal of responsibility, where one blames everyone apart from oneself, that I would like to turn to a recent and disturbing case. On 24 May 2014, Elliot Rodger, a 22-year-old student at Santa Barbara Community College killed six people and injured thirteen more before taking his own life in Isla Vista, California. His suicide note took two forms: a long video, shot in a couple of sunny locations in or beside his beautiful black BMW, and a much longer 137-page manifesto called 'My Twisted World'. I would urge the reader to watch the video, which is the very quintessence of narcissistic self-regard, and avoid the text, which I had the misfortune to read in its entirety. Rodger characterizes what he calls his 'Day of Retribution' in the following terms: 'Exacting my Retribution is my way of proving my true worth to the world.'

Rodger depicts himself as a brilliant, tortured and misunderstood hero whose suicide is not any expression of free will but a necessary act in order to avoid punishment after committing murder. In his manifesto, he recounts his life story in exhaustive and exhausting detail and documents the perceived difficulties he experienced because of his ethnicity, 'I am half white and half Asian, and this made it different from the normal fully white kids I was trying to fit in with.' He describes himself as starved of sex and unable to attract 'girls' (his word, not mine). His particular, recurring obsession is with blonde women at his college. In July 2013, he went to a party and started a fight after seeing a young woman talk to a young Asian man, 'How could an ugly Asian attract the attention of a white girl, while a beautiful Eurasian like myself never gets any attention from them.' In the fight his leg is broken and he complains that 'not one girl offered to help me as I stumbled home with a broken leg, beaten and bloody. If girls had been attracted to me ... they would have even offered to sleep with me to make me feel better.'

He planned his Day of Retribution with great care and precision, while at the same time meeting with his psychiatrist, who is (incredibly) called Dr Sophy.

Refusing the world of Sophy's philosophy, Rodger buys a bunch of handguns and ammunition, fantasizes about killing his stepmother and younger brother, but keeps delaying his date with destiny. The last paragraph of the manifesto reiterates his characterization of himself as the rightful actor and insists that the killing spree is a righting of wrongs: 'I am the true victim in all of this. I am the good guy. Humanity struck at me first by condemning me to experience so much suffering. I didn't ask for this. I didn't want this.'

Elliot Rodger is an extreme example, I know, but it shows how a highly elaborate suicide note, both as video and manifesto, can culminate in a total absence of any moral responsibility: 'I am a victim.' 'This is everyone else's fault.' 'You are to blame.' 'This is just retribution for what you did to me.' Suicide merges seamlessly with homicide as punishment for the wrongs perpetrated by one's parents, community and society as a whole. Rodger feels that the whole universe is against him and this utterly vindicates his actions. What is so breath-taking throughout his manifesto is his unquestioned and unflinching sense of entitlement.

One thinks, of course, of the Sandy Hook Elementary School shooting on 14 December 2012 in Newtown, Connecticut. After first shooting his mother, Nancy Lanza, with four gunshots to the head, Adam Lanza then used his mother's rifle to break into the school and kill twenty children and six adults before killing himself. All the children were aged between 6 and 7 years old. Although the State of Connecticut report, released on 25 November 2013, was unable to show any clear evidence as to the motive for Lanza's actions (aside from an obsession with mass shootings, like the Columbine high school shootings of 1999, and playing assorted violent, but widely available, video games like *Call of Duty* and *Grand Theft Auto*), I have an open question about the phenomenon of homicide-suicide. Has a new and extreme form of suicide as homicide begun to emerge over recent years where suicidal urges are increasingly transformed into homicidal rampages?

I guess only time will tell. Meanwhile, cases like those of Rodger and Lanza continue to proliferate. What is most depressing is that a simple change in US gun control legislation would make such incidents less likely, less bloody and considerably more difficult to perpetrate. Sadly, thanks to the powerful lobbying and deep pockets of the National Rifle Association, such wisdom seems to be beyond the capacity of the US Congress. In response to the rise of suicide as homicide, one is perversely inclined to plead for a return to good, old-fashioned self-killing: 'Sure, take yourself out if you insist, but please don't kill anyone else.'

¶ Suicide notes can also be disarmingly straightforward and honest. In his final two years, George Eastman, founder of Eastman Kodak, was in intense pain caused by a disorder affecting his spine. On 14 March 1932, Eastman shot himself in the heart, leaving a short note, 'To my friends: my work is done. Why wait?'

Four days before he shot himself, in 2005, the celebrated author and gonzo journalist Hunter S. Thompson wrote,

> Football season is over. No more games. No more
> bombs. No more walking. No more fun. No more
> swimming. 67. 17 years past 50. 17 more than I needed or
> wanted. Boring. I am always bitchy. No fun for anybody.

67, you are getting greedy. Act your old age. Relax. This won't hurt.

In notes like this and Eastman's, there is no revenge, retribution, entitlement, self-justification or even much self-pity. There is rather a sober lucidity and honesty that gives one pause and invites quiet admiration.

Which brings me back to my suicide note creative writing workshop, as I didn't recount the best part of the story. After I'd finished my little talk, I distributed small white index cards and invited everyone present to write their own suicide notes. People took to the task with great earnestness and silence descended for fifteen minutes, as the rain fell outside with occasional spots falling on the participants as they ruminated on their words. We then agreed that everyone could read out their note to the group, if they so wished. This was a genuinely surprising moment in the class. It was intensely moving.

Some people made jokes. A young woman wrote, 'I am sorry, mostly to my dog. Love Lauren. P.S. Please don't bury me in Los Angeles.' But another woman with a glowing complexion and a soft English accent addressed the following note to her children: 'When you inevitably discover those things I kept secret, let these not diminish the reality, nor the magnitude of my love for you.' The emphasis on love was present in many of the notes. My friend Nadja Agyropoulou wrote, 'I am so filled with love it is still too much to bear. I cannot find my way. The world is all wrong and although I withstood the worst of it, I lost out.' Never to be outdone, my wife, who also happens to be a psychoanalyst and therefore a specialist in ambivalence, wrote the following to me:

Dear Simon,

Break a leg, or all your legs. I better brake fast.

With all my love-hate,

Jamieson (who is about to drive us off a cliff)

Strangely enough, a few weeks after hearing this, I broke not my leg but my proximal humerus in four places.

A story about the class appeared a couple of days later in the *New York Times*, which was picked up separately by ABC News. Both stories were responsibly and carefully researched, but the online reaction was predictable in its outrage, claiming that I was being disrespectful of people who had suffered the suicide of their loved ones. All I can say is that this was not the mood in the room or the spirit of the little group that met on that wet Saturday afternoon. Others claimed that the project was stupid and self-centred, which is entirely possible. Someone wrote, 'Philosophy Professor makes STUDENTS NUTS', which I rather liked. But perhaps the proudest moment of my career was when the story got picked up and horribly mangled by the British tabloid press, notably the *Daily Mail*. By this time, the assumption had become that I was giving a semester-long course at The New School on suicide notes and students were required to pay fees (which, of course, they weren't). Someone tagged as 'Mary-3' exclaimed 'What a sick individual' and then I finally got the response I had been waiting for my whole life: 'This man should be sacked.'

The most powerful response to the class came via email from Terry Parke, a former Buddhist monk who became an atheist. He told me that he works as a licensed social worker with a lot of parasuicides – people who try and fail to kill themselves. He sent me an old suicide note from years back. It read simply: 'DARK. Light.

DARK'.

I failed to mention that, during the fifteen-minute period in the class when people were writing their suicide notes, I tried repeatedly, but no words would come. I just couldn't write anything down. I don't know why.

IV.

Death is not usually chosen as an end in itself, but for some other reason. As the evidence of suicide notes makes perfectly plain, people very often choose to die in order to avoid the unbearable pain caused by sickness, like cancer or Alzheimer's, or the intolerable psychical pain caused by severe depression, the tunnel vision of the melancholic, where all roads lead ineluctably to the same cul-de-sac. But, as we have also seen, suicide can be chosen for other reasons. One can choose to die for some cause that is believed to be greater than oneself, such as the innumerable cases of suicide bombing, self-immolation or starving oneself to death. Think of the death of hunger strikers like Bobby Sands amidst the degradation of the Maze Prison in Northern Ireland in 1981. Or consider the death of Simone Weil, who refused to eat more than the rations given to the citizens of France under German occupation. She died in self-starvation in a hospital in Ashford, England, in 1943. One can choose to die for a cause, for the sake of others: one's fellow soldiers, one's country, one's party, one's resistance movement or one's God. We have also seen how suicide can be chosen as a means of revenge, as a fatal payback for an experience of personal or collective betrayal. Suicide as revenge can fuel violent fantasies of persecution and victimization that can lead to grotesque acts of suicide as mass homicide.

But what if suicide is chosen for its own sake, because one simply wants to die? In a final series of reflections, I'd like to consider this question, which in many ways is much more frightening. If death is chosen because of some explicit cause, whether mental or corporeal, then we can empathize, seek to understand the particular predicament of the suicidal person and then quietly mutter under our breath, 'There but for the grace of God, go I.' But what if there is no apparent cause? What do we think then? And what, in such circumstances, would prevent us from taking our own lives? This is a more disturbing issue because it implies that someone like us, someone, let's say, who is just normally and boringly neurotic, but not suffering a fatal illness or clinical depression, could also choose to end their lives, right here and right now. We have seen the obvious philosophical flaws in all the arguments for and against suicide based on conceptions of rights or duties. So, what is stopping us? Why live?

In his short book, *Suicide*, the French writer and artist Edouard Levé tells the story of a 25-year-old man, born on 25 December (a kind of Christ figure, but that is rather too obvious a red herring), who is never named. The narrative is written in the second person singular, 'Since you seldom spoke, you were rarely wrong.' This has an effect that is at once impersonal and intimate, both chillingly distant and deeply personal. Having just left his house dressed for a tennis match with his wife, the 25-year-old claims he has forgotten something, turns back, walks down into his basement, picks up a shotgun and shoots himself in the head. Just before doing so, the young man had opened up a comic book to a specific page. This is his suicide note, which is overlooked because, before his gesture can be understood, his wife inadvertently closes the book and loses the page. Levé then killed himself ten days after handing in the manuscript to his publisher, on 15 October 2007. That's it.

Knowing this, we begin to search for meaning. Is the book a suicide note? Very possibly. The book's translator, Jan Steyn, rightly describes Levé's prose as stark and austere. But that cannot conceal the fact that the book is a love letter. To whom is it addressed? To the unnamed 25-year-old man? Or is it a love letter *from* the author *to* the author, from an older to a younger version of himself? Is it a kind of narcissistic loop? Perhaps. But we simply do not know and have to reconcile ourselves to this state of ignorance as we read Levé's love-hate story. Towards the end of the book, Levé writes, 'Are there good reasons for committing suicide? Those who survived you asked themselves these questions; they will not find answers.'

If Levé refuses to give us answers, what he does provide are some extraordinarily acute observations about suicide, again all written in the second person.

Only the living seem incoherent. Death closes the series of events that constitute their lives. So we resign ourselves to finding a meaning for them. To refuse them this would amount to accepting that a life, and thus life itself, is absurd. Yours had not yet attained the coherence of things done. Your death gave it this coherence.

One can understand this thought as a variety of the Sophoclean saying, 'Call no man happy until he is dead.' Namely, that the only guarantee of the happiness or blessedness of a life consists in the story that can be told about it after one's demise. Prior to that end, anything might happen and one might simply screw up. What the ancient Greeks called 'glory' consisted in the stories that could be told about one's noble or ignoble actions after one's death. Like it or not, life only ever has a partial coherence, and the atoms of an existence can pull apart at any moment because of the effects of fortune or the force of the past. We forget this at our peril.

What kind of coherence does suicide give to a life? Levé insists, 'Your suicide was the most important thing you ever said.' Yet suicide produces a peculiar inversion of biography, where all of one's acts are read backwards through the lens of one's last moment:

> Those who knew you reread each of your acts in the light of your last ... Isn't it peculiar how this final gesture inverts your biography? ... Your final second changed your life in the eyes of others.

This is unquestionably true. We cannot but see the life of, say, Paul Celan or Kurt Cobain through the optic of their final seconds. Think about it in a less heroic manner: if I decided to leave my hotel room right now and walk into the churning waves, then my entire life would be read through that moment. Would that make sense of my life? Not really. But could we avoid trying to make sense of my life in terms of that final act? Not really. And I imagine that the same would be true of you, dear reader. Suicide might grant life coherence, but only by robbing it of complexity by viewing it through the instant of one's death.

Suicide saddens the past and abolishes the future. Everything is melancholically viewed through the lens of one fatal moment. The closest we get to any suggestion of a motive for suicide on the part of Levé or his twenty-five-year-old protagonist are the final words, 'This selfishness of your suicide displeased you. But, all things considered, the lull of death won out over life's painful commotion.' Levé paints the picture of a withdrawn, silent and private young man, who liked to stay in his room and listen to music and read books. The twenty-five-year-old is also depicted as a gentle, attractive, loving and nonviolent soul, 'You directed toward yourself a violence that you did not feel towards others.

For them you reserved all your patience and tolerance.'
So, why did he kill himself? You will not find answers.

¶ Levé writes 'Dead, you are as alive as you are vivid,'
and 'Dead, you make me more alive.' He goes on, with
a pathos shaped by a formalistic restraint, 'Your disap-
pearance is so unacceptable that the following lunacy
was born along with it: a belief in your eternity.' And
here is the glaring and obvious paradox of Levé's work:
the book is about someone who decides to bring about
their own end written by someone who also brought
about their own end. But life is endlessly replayed as
art. In deciding to kill themselves, both the twenty-five-
year-old protagonist and Levé himself live eternally.
In dying, they live forever: like Hamlet, like the Mona
Lisa, like Mrs Ramsay. *Ars longa, vita brevis.*

This, of course, is the truth of Albert Camus's idea of
absurd creation, a notion explicitly refused by Levé. For
Camus, we inhabit an absurd universe: without hope,
without God, but still with the overwhelming presence
of sin. Such is the consequence of radical freedom for
Camus, which is neither a relief nor a joy, but rather a
bitterly acknowledged fact. Freedom is a fate from which
I can take flight, but which I can never escape. In *The
Myth of Sisyphus*, Camus's overriding argument is that
suicide is not a legitimate response to the absurd. What
is required is artistic creation in the face of the absurd.
As Nietzsche would have put it, we need art in order not
to die from the truth.

Absurd creation turns on the following thought:
'Accepting a life *without appeal*, one can also agree to
work and create *without appeal*.' In a situation of radical
freedom, without appeal to God, King, country or the

circumstances of one's birth, the absurd person does not claim to solve life's purported mysteries or grant a transcendent meaning to life, but to experience and describe what happens here below. 'Everything begins with lucid indifference', Camus writes. This allusion to indifference resonates with Camus's *The Outsider*, where the anti-hero, Meursault, faced with the prospect of beheading by the guillotine for the thoughtlessly racist killing of an unnamed 'Arab', concludes with the words, 'I opened myself for the first time to the tender indifference of the world.' He goes on, 'I understood that I had been happy and I was still happy.'

It is the combination of the words 'tender' with 'indifference' that is key here. For Camus, indifference does not lead to cynicism, but to an experience of the world that holds it at a certain distance, but which is open to both the world's beauty and brutality and which approaches it with tenderness and understanding. Whether he likes it or not, Levé has engaged in an act of absurd creation, an experience of suicide that long outlives death by transforming it into art. Perverse as it may seem, the same might be true of suicide notes: in marking and explaining the decision to end a life, they endlessly outlive it.

It is not at all clear to me that Camus's argument is sufficient to establish the illegitimacy of suicide and the idea of absurd creation can in no way justify any prohibition of self-killing. Indeed, I have always sensed a tension in Camus between the refusal of hope that is the premise of absurdity, and the hope that informs and infuses his idea of absurd creation. Camus risks giving us back in some new form what he had initially taken away. If suicide is not a legitimate response to the absurd, then absurd creation cannot be a definitive answer to Camus's opening question: is or is not life worth living?

Jean Améry (the *nom de plume* of the Austrian Hanns Mayer) accepts Camus's premise of an absurd universe but refuses his conclusion that absurd creation renders suicide illegitimate. Although voluntary death as a negation of life is arguably 'senseless', Améry says, the *decision* to kill oneself is not senseless: 'Aiming at death but not subservient to the anti-logic of death ...[the decision] is not only made in freedom but also brings real freedom to us.'

'In other words', he adds, 'we are standing before the question mark that is still behind the concept of the *freedom of the will*. ... [W]e have to take ourselves into a realm that lies beyond determinism and indeterminism.' Unlike Camus, Améry wants to acknowledge the legitimacy of the decision to take one's life in the name of freedom. In a long and moving passage, indelibly marked by his long experience of incarceration and brutal torture by the Germans during the Second World War, Améry writes,

For even potential suicides, when they approach the threshold of the leap, must show that they are up to the presumptions of life, otherwise they would not find their road to the open and would be like the concentration camp inmate who doesn't dare run against the electrified fence, would still like to gulp down his evening soup and then the hot acorn soup in the morning and again a turnip soup at noon, and on and on. Still: a requirement of life is here – and not only here – the demand to escape a life lacking in dignity, humanity, and freedom. And so death becomes life, just as from the moment of birth life is already a process of dying. And now negation all at once becomes something, even if good for nothing. Logic and dialectic

85

fail in tragicomic agreement. What counts is the option of
the subject.

As paradoxical as it might sound, the decision to end
one's life is a requirement of life in order to escape a
life of indignity and incarceration, the life of the concentration camp. Améry thus advocates respect for the
decision to kill oneself. He even argues for the beauty
of suicide, writing that 'Voluntary death is the privilege
of the human', and that 'a suicide is a *human being*. He
already belongs to the earth, but the earth still belongs
to him – and it is beautiful.'

The most strangely beautiful death note I've heard of
is the final radio communication with Donald Campbell
when he was attempting to beat the world water speed
record on Coniston Water in the Lake District in England
in 1967:

I'm hydra-floating, I'm hydra-floating
I'm going, I'm going, I'm gone.

Before shooting himself, a man wrote the following on a
piece of cardboard, 'Live fast, live well, die handsomely.'

Talk of the beauty of suicide might seem ethically
rebarbative to us. One finds the same thought in Levé
when he writes, 'Your death was scandalously beautiful.'
But we shouldn't give in to squeamishness just because
it conflicts with some contented, bovine moral worldview. We can have no idea of what Améry had to endure
during his torture and the trauma that followed and
therefore we should refrain from sanctimonious judg-
ments. But it seems to me that, as well as terror, there is
a strangely compulsive beauty to suicide, to the act, to
the leap. Just as there is sometimes a beauty to the dead,

to their stillness, their rest, their finally stopped character. Although this is hard to admit, I felt this when I saw my father's corpse about twenty minutes after he died almost exactly twenty years ago. His life was gone and finally his useless, meaningless suffering was over. He looked oddly beautiful. Small and shrunken, his skin brown and wrinkled, like some ancient wooden statue dug up from the earth.

¶ What I want to pick up on here, in closing, is Améry's idea that a suicide is a human being. Levé asks, 'Do plants commit suicide? Do animals die of hopelessness?' We don't know. Moreover, if we put those questions to plants and animals, then we probably wouldn't understand their response. Pea aphids, when threatened by a ladybug, can explode themselves, as can some species of termite. The Brazilian ant, *forelius pusillus*, engages in quasi-suicidal behaviour. Each night, as the ant nest is sealed, a number of ants remain outside to ensure that the seal is secure. They die before the nest is reopened the next morning. But this is not so much suicide as self-sacrifice for the greater ant, aphid or termite good. Perhaps it is the capacity for suicide, to make the decision for voluntary self-destruction, that picks us out as a species and distinguishes us as human.

This thought is picked up and pushed hard by one of the bleakest and most blackly humorous writers I know, the Romanian philosopher and aphorist, E. M. Cioran. In *A Short History of Decay*, Cioran writes,

> The man who has never imagined his own annihilation, who has not anticipated recourse to the rope, the bullet, poison or the sea, is a degraded galley slave or a worm

crawling upon the cosmic carrion. The world can take
everything from us, can forbid us everything, but no one
has the power to keep us from wiping ourselves out.

To be human is to have the capacity, at each and every
moment, of killing oneself. Incarceration, humiliation,
disappointment, disease – the world can do all of this
to us, but it cannot remove the possibility of suicide.
For as long as we keep this power in our hands, then we
are, in some minimal but real sense, free. Religions like
Christianity prohibit suicide because of the threat of insubordination that it poses: the refusal of the lordship
of God or King or Church or state. 'Suicide is one of
man's distinctive characteristics, one of his discoveries',
Cioran writes, 'no animal is capable of it, and the angels
have scarcely guessed its existence'. Suicide is like an
oxygen tank from which we can breathe in a world that
has become, in Hamlet's words, a prison. Cioran perversely concludes, 'Without suicide, no salvation.'

Is Cioran counselling that we should kill ourselves?
Not in the slightest. The idea that suicide is our salvation
does not entail that we should try and save ourselves
with the rope or the bullet. In *All Gall is Divided*, Cioran
writes that 'Only optimists commit suicide, the optimists
who can no longer be... optimists. The others, having no
reason to live, why should they have any to die?' The
'others' of whom Cioran speaks here are the pessimists,
amongst whom he counts himself. And here is the brilliance of this line of thought: there is finally something
too optimistic about suicide, too positive and assertive,
too caught up in the fantasy of salvation through death.
In the pleasingly entitled *The Trouble with Being Born*,
Cioran writes, 'When people come to me saying they
want to kill themselves, I tell them, "What's your rush?

You can kill yourself any time you like. So calm down. Suicide is a positive act." And they do calm down.'

Perhaps we have to calm down and look at matters more soberly and more pessimistically, without giving in to optimistic delusions that our death would solve any kind of problem, enact payback, revenge or retribution, save us from ourselves, from others or from the painful commotion of the world. In a delicious *coup de grâce*, Cioran writes, 'The refutation of suicide: is it not inelegant to abandon a world which has so willingly put itself at the service of our melancholy?'

I find something grimly reassuring and even fortifying in what we might call 'the inelegant refutation of suicide'. Let's grant that the capacity for suicide is what, at least partially, picks us out as a species. For as long as we are in possession of the powers of reflection and basic motility skills, we own the weapon with which we can assert our freedom and end our days, should we wish for such a consummation. But this does not entail that we should use that weapon. Not at all. That would be far too optimistic an act. Nothing would be saved by our suicide.

Why not calm down and enjoy the world's melancholy spectacle that spreads out so capaciously and delightfully before us? Why not linger a while in the face of what Nietzsche calls 'strict, hard factuality'? Why not try and turn our selves inside out, away from the finally hateful inward suffering, and outwards and upwards towards others, not in the name of some right or duty, but out of love? Each of us has the power to kill ourselves, but why not choose instead to give oneself to another or others in an act of love, that is, to give what one does not have and to receive that over which one has no power? Why not attempt a minimal conversion away from the self-aversion that lacerates and paralyzes us towards another possible version of ourselves? Is this not finally more courageous? Such is perhaps what Nietzsche calls the pessimism of strength as opposed to an optimism of naivety and weakness. True pessimists don't kill themselves. Is that not enough?

¶ It is enough. I would like to return to where I began, with waves, water and the sea. As is well known, in 1941, Virginia Woolf placed stones in her pockets and entered a river near her home in East Sussex, drowning herself, most Ophelia-like. Facing her fourth breakdown, complaining of hearing voices, and terrified of another descent into madness, Woolf wrote to her husband,

> I can't fight it any longer. I know that I am spoiling your life. ... You see I can't even write this properly. I can't read. What I want to say is I owe all the happiness of my life to you.

These words are marked by the same ambivalence that we saw in other suicide notes: an intense self-hatred combines with a profound expression of love.

But it is not the circumstance of Woolf's death that I want to dwell on. It is not Woolf's suicide that grants her life coherence. That coherence is provided by the courage of her work and what she wrote about life. This matters much more. I'd like to end by quoting a stunning passage from *To the Lighthouse*,

> Always, Mrs Ramsay felt, one helped oneself out of solitude reluctantly by laying hold of some little odd or end, some sound, some sight. She listened, but it was all very

still; cricket was over; the children were in their baths; there was only the sound of the sea. She stopped knitting; she held the long reddish-brown stocking dangling in her hands a moment. She saw the light again. With some irony in her interrogation, for when one woke at all, one's relations changed, she looked at the steady light, the pitiless, the remorseless, which was so much her, yet so little her, which had her at its beck and call (she woke in the night and saw it bent across their bed, stroking the floor), but for all that she thought, watching it with fascination, hypnotized, as if it were stroking with its silver fingers some sealed vessel in her brain whose bursting would flood her with delight, she had known happiness, exquisite happiness, intense happiness, and it silvered the rough waves a little more brightly, as daylight faded, and the blue went out of the sea and it rolled in waves of pure lemon which curved and swelled and broke upon the beach and the ecstasy burst in her eyes and waves of pure delight raced over the floor of her mind and she felt, It is enough! It is enough!

The topic of suicide immediately raises the following question: by virtue of what is or is not life meaningful? It might seem that if we cannot answer the question of life's meaning, then it would be prudent, perhaps even necessary, to exit life for... whatever: God or the void or some mixture of the two. If we cannot find reasons to be, then perhaps it is better not to be. But that would be a huge mistake, a fatal misstep. The question of life's meaning is an error and should simply be given up. The great revelation will never come. The clouds will never part with the promise of salvation and our minds will never stop rattling down through gutters of doubt, self-deceit, self-pity and guilt. Instead, thinking of Woolf again, there are little daily miracles, matches struck in the dark, the breaking waves, and Mrs. Ramsay saying 'Life stand still here.'

When life stands still here and we face the endless, shifting, indifferent grey-brown sea, when we hold ourselves open out into that indifference tenderly, without pining, self-pitying, complaining or expecting some reward or glittering prize, then we might have become, just for that moment, something that has endured and will endure, someone who can find some sort of sufficiency: right here, right now.

This moment, one out of a million, out of a million millions, towards 4.30 p.m. on a Thursday afternoon in late November, on this East Anglian beach, grey cloud, gulls, gusts of wind, vast darkness descending. Here is delight. Here one can help oneself out of one's solitude, shift that wedge-shaped core of darkness that is the self, and reach out and up towards another... in love.

Ecstasy bursts into our eyes. It is enough.

Aldeburgh, England
Sometime, near the end of 2014

93

Afterword

OF SUICIDE by DAVID HUME

1. One considerable advantage, that arises from philosophy, consists in the sovereign antidote, which it affords to superstition and false religion. All other remedies against that pestilent distemper are vain, or, at least, uncertain. Plain good-sense, and the practice of the world, which alone serve most purposes of life, are here found ineffectual: History, as well as daily experience, affords instances of men, endowed with the strongest capacity for business and affairs, who have all their lives crouched under slavery to the grossest superstition. Even gaiety and sweetness of temper, which infuse a balm into every other wound, afford no remedy to so virulent a poison; as we may particularly observe of the fair sex, who, tho' commonly possessed of these rich presents of nature, feel many of their joys blasted by this importunate intruder. But when sound philosophy has once gained possession of the mind, superstition is effectually excluded; and one may safely affirm, that her triumph over this enemy is more compleat than over most of the vices and imperfections, incident to human nature. Love or anger, ambition or avarice, have their root in the temper and affections, which the soundest reason is scarce ever able fully to correct. But superstition, being founded on false opinion, must immediately vanish, when true philosophy has inspired juster sentiments of superior powers. The contest is here more equal between the distemper and the medicine: And nothing can hinder the latter from proving effectual, but its being false and sophisticated.

2. It will here be superfluous to magnify the merits of philosophy, by displaying the pernicious tendency of that vice, of which it cures the human mind. The

superstitious man, says *Tully* [1], is miserable in every scene, in every incident of life. Even sleep itself, which banishes all other cares of unhappy mortals, affords to him matter of new terror; while he examines his dreams, and finds in those visions of the night, prognostications of future calamities. I may add, that, tho' death alone can put a full period to his misery, he dares not fly to this refuge, but still prolongs a miserable existence, from a vain fear, lest he offend his maker, by using the power, with which that beneficent being has endowed him. The presents of God and Nature are ravished from us by this cruel enemy; and notwithstanding that one step would remove us from the regions of pain and sorrow, her menaces still chain us down to a hated being, which she herself chiefly contributes to render miserable.

3. It is observed of such as have been reduced by the calamities of life to the necessity of employing this fatal remedy, that, if the unseasonable care of their friends deprive them of that species of death, which they proposed to themselves, they seldom venture upon any other, or can summon up so much resolution, a second time, as to execute their purpose. So great is our horror of death, that when it presents itself under any form, besides that to which a man has endeavoured to reconcile his imagination, it acquires new terrors, and overcomes his feeble courage. But when the menaces of superstition are joined to this natural timidity, no wonder it quite deprives men of all power over their lives; since even many pleasures and enjoyments, to which we are carried by a strong propensity, are torn

1. *De Divin*. lib. ii.

from us by this inhuman tyrant. Let us here endeavour to restore men to their native liberty, by examining all the common arguments against Suicide, and shewing, that that action may be free from every imputation of guilt or blame; according to the sentiments of all the ancient philosophers.

4. If Suicide be criminal, it must be a transgression of our duty, either to God, our neighbour, or ourselves.

5. To prove, that Suicide is no transgression of our duty to God, the following considerations may perhaps suffice. In order to govern the material world, the almighty creator has established general and immutable laws, by which all bodies, from the greatest planet to the smallest particle of matter, are maintained in their proper sphere and function. To govern the animal world, he has endowed all living creatures with bodily and mental powers; with senses, passions, appetites, memory, and judgment; by which they are impelled or regulated in that course of life, to which they are destined. These two distinct principles of the material and animal world continually encroach upon each other, and mutually retard or forward each other's operation. The powers of men and of all other animals are restrained and directed by the nature and qualities of the surrounding bodies; and the modifications and actions of these bodies are incessantly altered by the operation of all animals. Man is stopped by rivers in his passage over the surface of the earth; and rivers, when properly directed, lend their force to the motion of machines, which serve to the use of man. But tho' the provinces of the material and animal powers are not kept entirely separate, there result from thence no

discord or disorder in the creation: On the contrary, from the mixture, union, and contrast of all the various powers of inanimate bodies and living creatures, arises that surprising harmony and proportion, which affords the surest argument of supreme wisdom.

6. The providence of the deity appears not immediately in any operation, but governs every thing by those general and immutable laws, which have been established from the beginning of time. All events, in one sense, may be pronounced the action of the almighty: They all proceed from those powers, with which he has endowed his creatures. A house, which falls by its own weight, is not brought to ruin by his providence more than one destroyed by the hands of men; nor are the human faculties less his workmanship than the laws of motion and gravitation. When the passions play, when the judgment dictates, when the limbs obey; this is all the operation of God; and upon these animate principles, as well as upon the inanimate, has he established the government of the universe.

7. Every event is alike important in the eyes of that infinite being, who takes in, at one glance, the most distant regions of space and remotest periods of time. There is no one event, however important to us, which he has exempted from the general laws that govern the universe, or which he has peculiarly reserved for his own immediate action and operation. The revolutions of states and empires depend upon the smallest caprice or passion of single men; and the lives of men are shortened or extended by the smallest accident of air or diet, sunshine or tempest. Nature still continues her progress and operation; and if general laws be ever

broke by particular volitions of the deity, it is after
a manner which entirely escapes human observation.
As on the one hand, the elements and other inanimate
parts of the creation carry on their action without
regard to the particular interest and situation of men; so
men are entrusted to their own judgment and discretion
in the various shocks of matter, and may employ every
faculty, with which they are endowed,
in order to provide for their ease, happiness,
or preservation.

8. What is the meaning, then, of that principle, that a
man, who, tired of life, and hunted by pain and misery,
bravely overcomes all the natural terrors of death, and
makes his escape from this cruel scene; that such a
man, I say, has incurred the indignation of his creator,
by encroaching on the office of divine providence, and
disturbing the order of the universe? Shall we assert,
that the Almighty has reserved to himself, in any
peculiar manner, the disposal of the lives of men, and
has not submitted that event, in common with others,
to the general laws, by which the universe is governed?
This is plainly false. The lives of men depend upon the
same laws as the lives of all other animals; and these are
subjected to the general laws of matter and motion. The
fall of a tower or the infusion of a poison will destroy a
man equally with the meanest creature: An inundation
sweeps away every thing, without distinction, that
comes within the reach of its fury. Since therefore the
lives of men are for ever dependent on the general
laws of matter and motion; is a man's disposing of his
life criminal, because, in every case, it is criminal to
encroach upon these laws, or disturb their operation?
But this seems absurd. All animals are entrusted to

their own prudence and skill for their conduct in the world, and have full authority, as far as their power extends, to alter all the operations of nature. Without the exercise of this authority, they could not subsist a moment. Every action, every motion of a man innovates in the order of some parts of matter, and diverts, from their ordinary course,
the general laws of motion. Putting together, therefore, these conclusions, we find, *that* human life depends upon the general laws of matter and motion, and *that* it is no encroachment on the office of providence to disturb or alter these general laws. Has not every one, of consequence, the free disposal of his own life? And may he not lawfully employ that power with which nature has endowed him?

9. In order to destroy the evidence of this conclusion, we must shew a reason, why this particular case is excepted. Is it because human life is of so great importance, that it is a presumption for human prudence to dispose of it? But the life of man is of no greater importance to the universe than that of an oyster. And were it of ever so great importance, the order of nature has actually submitted it to human prudence, and reduced us to a necessity, in every incident, of determining concerning it.

10. Were the disposal of human life so much reserved as the peculiar province of the almighty that it were an encroachment on his right for men to dispose of their own lives; it would be equally criminal to act for the preservation of life as for its destruction. If I turn aside a stone, which is falling upon my head, I disturb the course of nature, and I invade the peculiar province

of the almighty, by lengthening out my life, beyond
the period, which, by the general laws of matter and
motion, he had assigned to it.

11. A hair, a fly, an insect is able to destroy this
mighty being, whose life is of such importance. Is it
an absurdity to suppose, that human prudence may
lawfully dispose of what depends on such insignificant
causes?

12. It would be no crime in me to divert the *Nile* or
Danube from its course, were I able to effect such
purposes. Where then is the crime of turning a few
ounces of blood from their natural chanels!

13. Do you imagine that I repine at providence or
curse my creation, because I go out of life, and put a
period to a being, which, were it to continue, would
render me miserable? Far be such sentiments from
me. I am only convinced of a matter of fact, which you
yourself acknowledge possible, that human life may be
unhappy, and that my existence, if farther prolonged,
would become uneligible. But I thank providence,
both for the good, which I have already enjoyed, and
for the power, with which I am endowed, of escaping
the ill that threatens me[2]. To you it belongs to repine
at providence, who foolishly imagine that you have no
such power, and who must still prolong a hated being,
tho' loaded with pain and sickness, with shame and
poverty.

14. Do you not teach, that when any ill befalls me, tho'
by the malice of my enemies, I ought to be resigned
to providence; and that the actions of men are the

102

operations of the almighty as much as the actions of inanimate beings? When I fall upon my own sword, therefore, I receive my death equally from the hands of the deity, as if it had proceeded from a lion, a precipice, or a fever.

15. The submission, which you require to providence, in every calamity, that befalls me, excludes not human skill and industry; if possibly, by their means, I can avoid or escape the calamity. And why may I not employ one remedy as well as another?

16. If my life be not my own, it were criminal for me to put it in danger, as well as to dispose of it: Nor could one man deserve the appellation of *Hero*, whom glory or friendship transports into the greatest dangers, and another merit the reproach of *Wretch* or *Miscreant*, who puts a period to his life, from the same or like motives.

17. There is no being, which possesses any power or faculty, that it receives not from its creator; nor is there any one, which, by ever so irregular an action, can encroach upon the plan of his providence, or disorder the universe. Its operations are his work equally with that chain of events, which it invades; and which ever principle prevails, we may, for that very reason, conclude it to be most favoured by him. Be it animate or inanimate, rational or irrational, it is all a case: Its power is still derived from the supreme creator, and is alike comprehended in the order of his providence. When the horror of pain prevails over the love of life: When a voluntary action anticipates the effect of blind

2. *Agamus Deo gratias, quod nemo in vita teneri potest.* Seneca, *Epist.*xii.

causes; it is only in consequence of those powers and
principles, which he has implanted in his creatures.
Divine providence is still inviolate, and placed far
beyond the reach of human injuries.

18. It is impious, says the old *Roman* superstition[3],
to divert rivers from their course, or invade the
prerogatives of nature. It is impious, says the *French*
superstition, to inoculate for the small-pox, or usurp
the business of providence, by voluntarily producing
distempers and maladies. It is impious, says the modern
European superstition, to put a period to our own life,
and thereby rebel against our creator. And why not
impious, say I, to build houses, cultivate the ground,
and sail upon the ocean? In all these actions, we employ
our powers of mind and body to produce
some innovation in the course of nature; and in none
of them do we any more. They are all of them,
therefore, equally innocent or equally criminal.

19. *But you are placed by providence, like a sentinel, in a
particular station; and when you desert it, without being
recalled, you are guilty of rebellion against your almighty
sovereign, and have incurred his displeasure.* I ask, why do
you conclude, that Providence has placed me in this
station? For my part, I find, that I owe my birth to
a long chain of causes, of which many and even the
principal, depended upon voluntary actions of men.
*But Providence guided all these causes, and nothing happens in
the universe without its consent and co-operation.* If so, then
neither does my death, however voluntary, happen
without its consent; and whenever pain and sorrow so
far overcome my patience as to make me tired of life, I

3. *Tacit. Ann.* lib. i.

may conclude, that I am recalled from my station, in the clearest and most express terms.

20. It is providence, surely, that has placed me at present in this chamber: But may I not leave it, when I think proper, without being liable to the imputation of having deserted my post or station? When I shall be dead, the principles, of which I am composed, will still perform their part in the universe, and will be equally useful in the grand fabric, as when they composed this individual creature. The difference to the whole will be no greater than between my being in a chamber and in the open air. The one change is of more importance to me than the other; but not more so to the universe.

21. It is a kind of blasphemy to imagine, that any created being can disturb the order of the world, or invade the business of providence. It supposes, that that being possesses powers and faculties, which it received not from its creator, and which are not subordinate to his government and authority. A man may disturb society, no doubt; and thereby incur the displeasure of the almighty: But the government of the world is placed far beyond his reach and violence. And how does it appear, that the almighty is displeased with those actions, that disturb society? By the principles which he has implanted in human nature, and which inspire us with a sentiment of remorse, if we ourselves have been guilty of such actions, and with that of blame and disapprobation, if we ever observe them in others. Let us now examine, according to the method proposed, whether Suicide be of this kind of actions, and be a breach of our duty to our *neighbour* and to society.

22. A man, who retires from life, does no harm to society. He only ceases to do good; which, if it be an injury, is of the lowest kind.

23. All our obligations to do good to society seem to imply something reciprocal. I receive the benefits of society, and therefore ought to promote its interest. But when I withdraw myself altogether from society, can I be bound any longer?

24. But allowing, that our obligations to do good were perpetual, they have certainly some bounds. I am not obliged to do a small good to society, at the expence of a great harm to myself. Why then should I prolong a miserable existence, because of some frivolous advantage, which the public may, perhaps, receive from me? If upon account of age and infirmities, I may lawfully resign any office, and employ my time altogether in fencing against these calamities, and alleviating, as much as possible, the miseries of my future life: Why may I not cut short these miseries at once by an action, which is no more prejudicial to society?

25. But suppose, that it is no longer in my power to promote the interest of the public: Suppose, that I am a burthen to it: Suppose, that my life hinders some person from being much more useful to the public. In such cases my resignation of life must not only be innocent but laudable. And most people, who lie under any temptation to abandon existence, are in some such situation. Those, who have health, or power, or authority, have commonly better reason to be in humour with the world.

26. A man is engaged in a conspiracy for the public interest; is seized upon suspicion; is threatened with the rack; and knows, from his own weakness, that the secret will be extorted from him: Could such a one consult the public interest better than by putting a quick period to a miserable life? This was the case of the famous and brave *Strozzi* of *Florence*.

27. Again, suppose a malefactor justly condemned to a shameful death; can any reason be imagined, why he may not anticipate his punishment, and save himself all the anguish of thinking on its dreadful approaches? He invades the business of providence no more than the magistrate did, who ordered his execution; and his voluntary death is equally advantageous to society, by ridding it of a pernicious member.

28. That Suicide may often be consistent with interest and with our duty to *ourselves*, no one can question, who allows, that age, sickness, or misfortune may render life a burthen, and make it worse even than anni-hilation. I believe that no man ever threw away life, while it was worth keeping. For such is our natural horror of death, that small motives will never be able to reconcile us to it. And tho' perhaps the situation of a man's health or fortune did not seem to require this remedy, we may at least be assured, that any one, who, without apparent reason, has had recourse to it, was curst with such an incurable depravity or gloominess of temper, as must poison all enjoyment, and render him equally miserable as if he had been loaded with the most grievous misfortunes.

29. If Suicide be supposed a crime, it is only cowardice

can impel us to it. If it be no crime, both prudence and courage should engage us to rid ourselves at once of existence, when it becomes a burthen. It is the only way, that we can then be useful to society, by setting an example, which, if imitated, would preserve to every one his chance for happiness in life, and would effectually free him from all danger of misery[4].

4. It would be easy to prove, that Suicide is as lawful under the *Christian* dispensation as it was to the heathens. There is not a single text of scripture, which prohibits it. That great and infallible rule of faith and practice, which must control all philosophy and human reasoning, has left us, in this particular, to our natural liberty. Resignation to providence is, indeed, recommended in scripture; but that implies only submission to ills, which are unavoidable, not to such as may be remedied by prudence or courage. *Thou shalt not kill* is evidently meant to exclude only the killing of others, over whose life we have no authority. That this precept like most of the scripture precepts, must be modified by reason and common sense, is plain from the practice of magistrates, who punish criminals capitally, notwithstanding the letter of this law. But were this commandment ever so express against Suicide, it could now have no authority. For all the law of *Moses* is abolished, except so far as it is established by the law of nature; and we have already endeavoured to prove, that Suicide is not prohibited by that law. In all cases, *Christians* and *Heathens* are precisely upon the same footing; and if *Cato* and *Brutus*, *Arria* and *Portia* acted heroically, those who now imitate their example ought to receive the same praises from posterity. The power of committing Suicide is regarded by *Pliny* as an advantage which men possess even above the deity himself. *Deus non sibi potest mortem consciscere, si velit, quod homini dedit optimum in tantis vitae poenis*. Lib. ii. Cap. 7.

Sources & Acknowledgments

As I haven't included any footnotes in this book,
for ease of reading, I'd like to give a brief indication
of sources used. Marc Etkind's *Or Not to Be* has long
been invaluable for thinking about the history of
suicide notes and Michael Cholbi's essay on 'Suicide'
for the *Stanford Encyclopedia of Philosophy* is a brilliant
raccourci of the main lines of philosophical debate on
the question of suicide from the standpoint of moral
philosophy. I plundered from both texts. I'd like to
thank Manya Lempert for alerting me to passages from
Virginia Woolf. I went back to some material from my
The Book of Dead Philosophers, and an old, unpublished
manuscript by Silvia Berti's on Radicati di Passerano.
Aside from my own reading, I'd like to thank Sarah
Schweig and Megan Beyer for their invaluable help
with background research on this project, particularly
in the areas of literature, law, sociology and innumerable factoids. Much of this wasn't included, but it was
nonetheless invaluable. I'd like to thank Nemonie
Craven for her help and advice,and Jacques Testard for
his careful editing of the text.

For the preface to the revised edition, I made reference
to the following sources: Kay Redfield Jamison, *Night
Falls Fast*; Andrew Solomon, *The Noonday Demon*;
Virginia Heffernan, *Magic and Loss*; and to two ongoing semi-open-source literature reviews by Jonathan
Haidt and Jean Twenge: 'Social Media Use and Mental
Health: A Review', and 'Is There an Increase in
Adolescent Mood Disorders, Self-Harm, and Suicide
Since 2010 in the USA and UK? A Review'. I would
also like to thank heartily the readers of the original
edition who contacted me over the years. They asked
questions, shared thoughts, and, in many cases, trusted
me with their personal stories and struggles with

suicide. I learned a great deal. I have corrected errors and sharpened a few sentences, but the text of this revised edition is substantially unchanged.

Also published by Fitzcarraldo Editions

Zone by Mathias Enard (Fiction)
Translated from French by Charlotte Mandell
'A modern masterpiece.'
— David Collard, *Times Literary Supplement*

Memory Theatre by Simon Critchley (Essay)
'A brilliant one-of-a-kind mind-game occupying a strange
frontier between philosophy, memoir and fiction.'
— David Mitchell, author of *The Bone Clocks*

On Immunity by Eula Biss (Essay)
'A vaccine against vague and incoherent thinking.'
— Rebecca Solnit, author of *Wanderlust: A History of Walking*

My Documents by Alejandro Zambra (Fiction)
Translated from Spanish by Megan McDowell
'Strikingly original.'
— James Wood, *New Yorker*

It's No Good by Kirill Medvedev (Essay)
Introduced by Keith Gessen
Translated by Keith Gessen, Mark Krotov, Cory Merrill
and Bela Shayevich
'Russia's first authentic post-Soviet writer.'
— Keith Gessen, co-founder of *n+1*

Street of Thieves by Mathias Enard (Fiction)
Translated by Charlotte Mandell
'This is what the great contemporary French novel should
be. ... Enard fuses the traditions of Camus and Céline, but
he is his own man.'
— Patrick McGuinness, author of *The Last Hundred Days*

Pond by Claire-Louise Bennett (Fiction)
'An extraordinary collection of short stories – profoundly original though not eccentric, sharp and tender, funny and deeply engaging. A very new sort of writing...'
— Sara Maitland, author of *A Book of Silence*

Nicotine by Gregor Hens (Essay)
Introduced by Will Self
Translated by Jen Calleja
'A luminous and nuanced exploration of how we're constituted by our obsessions, how our memories arrange themselves inside of us, and how – or if – we control our own lives.'
— Leslie Jamison, author of *The Empathy Exams*

Nocilla Dream by Agustín Fernandez Mallo (Fiction)
Translated by Thomas Bunstead
'An encyclopedia, a survey, a deranged anthropology. *Nocilla Dream* is just the cold-hearted poetics that might see America for what it really is – a testament to the brilliance of Agustín Fernández Mallo.'
— Ben Marcus, author of *The Flame Alphabet*

Pretentiousness: Why it Matters by Dan Fox (Essay)
'A lucid and impassioned defence of thinking, creating and, ultimately, living in a world increasingly dominated by the massed forces of social and intellectual conservatism.'
— Tom McCarthy, author of *Satin Island*

Counternarratives by John Keene (Fiction)
'Keene's collection of short and longer historical fictions are formally varied, mould-breaking, and deeply political. He's a radical artist working in the most conservative genres, and any search for innovation in this year's US fiction should start here.'
— Christian Lorentzen, *Vulture*

Second-hand Time by Svetlana Alexievich (Essay)
Translated by Bela Shayevich
'*Second-hand Time* is her most ambitious work: many women and a few men talk about the loss of the Soviet idea, the post-Soviet ethnic wars, the legacy of the Gulag, and other aspects of the Soviet experience.'
— Masha Gessen, *New Yorker*

The Hatred of Poetry by Ben Lerner (Essay)
'Lerner argues with the tenacity and the wildness of the vital writer and critic that he is. Each sentence of *The Hatred of Poetry* vibrates with uncommon and graceful lucidity; each page brings the deep pleasures of crisp thought, especially the kind that remains devoted to complexity rather than to its diminishment.'
— Maggie Nelson, author of *The Argonauts*

A Primer for Cadavers by Ed Atkins (Fiction)
'The most imaginative, sincere, and horribly, gloriously intent contemporary writer – certainly from Britain – I've read.'
— Sam Riviere, *Poetry London*

Bricks and Mortar by Clemens Meyer (Fiction)
Translated from German by Katy Derbyshire
'This is a wonderfully insightful, frank, exciting and heart-breaking read. *Bricks and Mortar* is like diving into a Force 10 gale of reality, full of strange voices, terrible events and a vision of neoliberal capitalism that is chillingly accurate.'
— A. L. Kennedy, author of *Serious Sweet*

Nocilla Experience by Agustín Fernandez Mallo (Fiction)
Translated from Spanish by Thomas Bunstead
'The best novel I read in 2016. Thrillingly, incandescently brilliant.'
— Stuart Evers, author of *The Blind Light*

The Doll's Alphabet by Camilla Grudova (Fiction)
'That I cannot say what all these stories are about is a
testament to their worth. They have been haunting me for
days now. They have their own, highly distinct flavour, and
the inevitability of uncomfortable dreams.'
— Nick Lezard, *Guardian*

This Young Monster by Charlie Fox (Essay)
'Good God, where did this wise-beyond-his-years 25-year-
old critic's voice come from? His breath of proudly putrefied
air is really something to behold. Finally, a new Parker Tyler
is on the scene. Yep. Mr. Fox is the real thing.'
— John Waters, *New York Times*

Compass by Mathias Enard (Fiction)
Translated from French by Charlotte Mandell
'One of the finest European novels in recent memory.'
— Adrian Nathan West, *Literary Review*

Notes from No Man's Land by Eula Biss (Essay)
'The most accomplished book of essays anyone has written
or published so far in the twenty-first century.'
— Kyle Minor, *Salon*

Flights by Olga Tokarczuk (Fiction)
Translated from Polish by Jennifer Croft
'Olga Tokarczuk is a household name in Poland and one
of Europe's major humanist writers, working here in the
continental tradition of the "thinking" or essayistic novel.
Flights has echoes of W. G. Sebald, Milan Kundera, Danilo
Kiš and Dubravka Ugrešić, but Tokarzcuk inhabits a
rebellious, playful register very much her own. ... Hotels on
the continent would do well to have a copy of *Flights* on the
bedside table. I can think of no better travel companion in
these turbulent, fanatical times.'
— Kapka Kassabova, *Guardian*

Essayism by Brian Dillon (Essay)
'A wonderful, subtle and deceptively fragmentary little book
... enjoyably roundabout and light-fingered ... To borrow
from one of Barthes's titles, this is a lover's discourse, the
love object being writing, not only in the essay but in all
its forms. It is also a testament to the consolatory, even the
healing, powers of art. And at the last, in its consciously
diffident fashion – Dillon is a literary flaneur in the tradition
of Baudelaire and Walter Benjamin – it is its own kind of
self-made masterpiece.'
—— John Banville, *Irish Times*

Moving Kings by Joshua Cohen (Fiction)
'A Jewish Sopranos... burly with particularities and
vibrant with voice... utterly engrossing, full of passionate
sympathy... This is a book of brilliant sentences, brilliant
paragraphs, brilliant chapters... There's not a page without
some vital charge — a flash of metaphor, an idiomatic
originality, a bastard neologism born of nothing... Cohen
is an extraordinary prose stylist, surely one of the most
prodigious in American fiction today... his sentences are
all-season journeyers, able to do everything everywhere at
once... A crystalline novelist with a journalistic openness to
the world.'
—— James Wood, *New Yorker*

Companions by Christina Hesselholdt (Fiction)
Translated from Danish by Paula Russell Garrett
'Hesselholdt's touch is light, even mocking, as much as
her subject matter is grave. There is a dancing intelligence
roaming free here, darting back and forth among ideas and
sensations. Her novel is a deceptively nonchalant defence of
modernism and a work of pure animation.'
—— Catherine Taylor, *Financial Times*

Fitzcarraldo Editions
8-12 Creekside
London SE8 3DX
United Kingdom

ISBN 978-1-9106950-6-7

Design by Ray O'Meara
Typeset in Fitzcarraldo
Printed and bound by TJ International

fitzcarraldoeditions.com

Fitzcarraldo Editions